Entrusted for Eternity

MIKE KEYES SR.

WORD & SPIRIT
PUBLISHING

Unless otherwise indicated, all Scripture quotes are from the New King James Version of the Bible. © 1982 by Thomas Nelson, Inc. All rights reserved.

Entrusted for Eternity
Copyright © 2025 by Mike Keyes Sr.
ISBN: 978-1-685730-73-4

Published by Word and Spirit Publishing
P.O. Box 701403
Tulsa, Oklahoma 74170
wordandspiritpublishing.com

Printed in the United States of America. All rights reserved under International Copyright Law. Content and/or cover may not be reproduced in whole or in part in any form without the expressed written consent of the Publisher.

Whatever you do in word or deed, do all in the name of the Lord Jesus, giving thanks to God the Father through Him.

—Colossians 3:17

And whatever you do, do it **heartily, as to the Lord** and not to men, knowing that from the Lord you will receive the reward of the inheritance; for you serve the Lord Christ.

—Colossians 3:23-24

And say to Archippus, "**Take heed** to the ministry which you have received in the Lord, that you may fulfill it."

—Colossians 4:17

Contents

Foreword vii

PART ONE: THE REALITY

CHAPTER 1: THE JOURNEY TO FOREVER 1
CHAPTER 2: ONE QUESTION CHANGED MY LIFE 9
CHAPTER 3: PARTNERSHIP BY DIVINE CHOICE 13
CHAPTER 4: ETERNAL DESTINATIONS 19

PART TWO: THE RESPONSIBILITY

CHAPTER 5: ENTRUSTED WITH THE GOSPEL 33
CHAPTER 6: ENTRUSTED WITH STEWARDSHIP 41
CHAPTER 7: ENTRUSTED WITH GOD'S PEOPLE 53
CHAPTER 8: ENTRUSTED TO BE LEAN, MEAN, AND CLEAN ... 61
CHAPTER 9: ENTRUSTED WITH THE WORK OF DISCIPLINE 69
CHAPTER 10: ENTRUSTED TO REPLICATE 77
CHAPTER 11: ENTRUSTED WITH FREE WILL 83
CHAPTER 12: ENTRUSTED WITH VERBAL POWER 89
CHAPTER 13: ENTRUSTED WITH AUTHORITY 95
CHAPTER 14: ENTRUSTED WITH WEAPONS OF WAR 101
CHAPTER 15: ENTRUSTED WITH LIFE 111
CHAPTER 16: ENTRUSTED WITH PURPOSE 121
CHAPTER 17: ENTRUSTED TO TRUST 147

PART THREE: THE HONOR

CHAPTER 18: THE UNKNOWN SOMEBODY 155
CHAPTER 19: THE LENGTH OF THE LINE 177
CHAPTER 20: MARILYN'S LINE 183
CHAPTER 21: BARBARA'S LINE 189
CHAPTER 22: MAC'S LINE 199
CHAPTER 23: NORVEL'S LINE 205
CHAPTER 24: WHOSE LINE WILL YOU STAND IN? 209
CHAPTER 25: WALKING WORTHY 213
CHAPTER 26: THE THANKFUL HEART 219
CHAPTER 27: INTENSITY IS INSPIRATIONAL 233
CHAPTER 28: PROMISES TO LIVE BY 245

Foreword

If you've read any of my previous books, you know that the underlying theme with all of them has been evangelism, spiritual warfare, military mentality, and the like. With that being said, I believe this book has been reserved by God to be written for such a time as this. I believe it is the most focused of all those that I've been graced by God to write. That one word, *entrusted*, has just exploded inside my heart. It is all at once magnificent, unnerving, and sobering to the core. It demands our blood, sweat, and tears as believers. It tells us why we Christians, once saved, remain on battlefield Earth until the day of our earthly departure. It reveals the awesome honor and responsibility given by God to all of His children in this life.

That one word: *entrusted!* After more than 4 decades of service in the army of the Lord, this word means more to me now than it ever has. As I look out at the ripe harvest fields of the world, it compels me, drives me, and defines me. You are just as entrusted with the gospel as I am. Have you taken the time to contemplate the eternal truth about heaven and hell, life and death? If not, perhaps this book's content will change that if in your life it needs to be changed. My prayer is that as you read the contents of this book, you'll awaken, or reawaken, to the

Entrusted for Eternity

sacred privilege handed to us by our Heavenly Father in these last days. **We're entrusted with the gospel, that means we must be responsible, available, and accountable.**

> When someone has been given much, much will be required in return; and when someone has been **entrusted** with much, even more will be required.
>
> —Luke 12:48b NLT

PART ONE:

THE REALITY

CHAPTER 1

THE JOURNEY TO FOREVER

For God so loved the world that He gave His only begotten son, that whoever believes in Him should not perish, but have **everlasting life**.

—John 3:16

... In flaming fire taking vengeance on those who do not know God, and on those who do not obey the gospel of our Lord Jesus Christ. These shall be punished with **everlasting destruction** *from the presence of the Lord and from the glory of His power.*

—2 Thessalonians 1: 8-9

Everlasting life. Everlasting death. *Everlasting means no change in condition, status, or location. Forever!* The truth that these are the only two eternal destinations for every human being is staggering in its reality. Wonderful beyond words for those who will experience everlasting life in heaven. Horrible beyond imagination for those who die lost in their sins and endure everlasting destruction.

I was saved at the age of 26. Ever since, the truth about eternity has been the one driving force that has kept me in my lane, running the assigned race God has given me to run. Like you and like all of us, I've made plenty of mistakes along life's racecourse, but no matter how many times the devil's hurdles and obstacles tripped me up, I've always been able by God's mercy and grace to get back up and resume running my race for Jesus. Why? Because of the truth about eternity. I stay focused on the finish line, thankful every day for God's mercy, forgiveness, and grace.

Turning away from Jesus will never happen in my life because I am very much aware of what He did to save me—and I am eternally thankful for it. I know what awaits each one of us after death, and so do you if you read the Bible. Therefore, I keep running for Jesus, and I pray you do, too. It is that way with me now, and will be that way until the day I step off planet Earth and go home to serve my Lord and Savior face to face—for all eternity.

Oh, give thanks to the Lord, for He is good! And His mercy **endures forever***.*

—Psalms 107:1.

BE ONE OF THE FEW

On the other hand, I am constantly amazed at how so few fellow believers live each day in the light of eternity. I honestly don't understand the lukewarmness all around me in the Body of Christ. I cherish the relationships I do have with like-minded believers and ministers, but the vast majority of saints just don't live like they know what's out there beyond the grave. The Lord compels me to write and exhort children of God everywhere once again. In my altar calls I've always emphasized the fact that there are no parole board hearings in hell, and will continue to do so. Why? Because the Bible is very clear on this subject. The sin of rejecting God's free gift of salvation brings eternal judgment upon the sinner. People who die without Christ face eternity with no hope of ever getting out of the lake of fire (Revelation 20:10-15).

> ... *That at that time you were without Christ, being aliens from the commonwealth of Israel and strangers from the covenants of promise, **having no hope** and without God in the world.*
>
> —Ephesians 2:12

This is the reality for an unbeliever who dies without Christ. They have absolutely no hope for a reversal of God's judgment and punishment. Never forget: the devil invented sin. In John 8:44, Jesus called him the *father* of lies, and as a result, the inventor of evil. The Bible says he was the most beautiful of all the creatures God created, *until iniquity was found in him* (Ezekiel 28:15). Hell was originally created for the devil and all those beings who follow him (Matthew 25:41). They made their choice eons ago, and have been sentenced accordingly. Their eternal punishment and suffering are sealed.

However, their place of eternal fire and punishment was never intended to be the final abode for people. But because God gives us all free will and the power of choice, men and women can sentence themselves to the same fate. Read and heed the contents of Revelation Chapter 20. All evil will one day be judged. Whether it be angelic, demonic, or human—every spirit who chooses rebellion against God will be punished eternally in everlasting fire. That's divine justice, and it *will* prevail. The good news for the living is this: judgment hasn't yet been set. As long as there is breath in our lungs, we can say the words that change our destiny and seal our salvation.

> I call heaven and earth as witnesses today against you, that I have set before you life and death, blessing and cursing; therefore **choose life**, that both you and your descendants may live.
>
> —Deuteronomy 30:19

> But I say to you that for **every idle word** men may speak, they will give account of it in the day of judgment. For by **your words** you will be **justified**, and by **your words** you will be **condemned**.
>
> —Matthew 12:36-37

> How then shall they call on Him in whom they have not believed? And how shall they believe in Him of whom they have not heard? And how shall they hear without a preacher? And how shall they preach unless they are sent? As it is written: "How beautiful are the feet of those who preach the gospel of peace, Who bring **glad tidings of good things**!"
>
> —Romans 10:14-15

We can change. We can repent. We can come clean, receive forgiveness, and become born again. It's up to each one of us, but somebody has to carry the good news that tells us how and why. That "somebody" is us—the Body of Christ, the Church. God so loved the world He sent Jesus to die in our place and make the way possible for us to receive salvation by faith (John 3:16). With words we declare our own eternal destination. With words we present this truth to the world. With words the people either accept or reject God's offer. Our words will be used as the criteria for eternal salvation or eternal damnation. *Words matter.*

OTHERS HAVE BEEN TOLD TO TELL

There are many books written by authors who have been taken to both heaven and hell to see, record, and share their experiences with us. I recommend several that I have in my library. The first one is Richard Sigmund's book, *My Time in Heaven*. Most of his book deals with his tour of heaven, describing the things he saw and people he met. It brings tears of joy to the reader, as he describes what is waiting for Christians after physical death. But there is one chapter where Jesus takes him down to the "place of separation." Reading that chapter is beyond sobering—it's terrifying. It was terrifying for him, and its terrifying for those who read what he saw down there.

That one chapter carries more weight with me than reading about all the joy, bliss, and rewards awaiting a Christian when they pass on from this life to eternity in heaven. I have read over that one chapter many times, and continue to do so as often as needed to keep things in perspective down here. Many others were also taken into that horrible place and have been instructed to write extensively about what they saw and felt. Mary Baxter's book, *A Divine Revelation of Hell*, and Bill Weisse's book, *23 Minutes in Hell*, are two in my library I strongly recommend you get these books, and others like them. They need to be read as often as necessary, to keep proper perspective day by day as we move towards our day of earthly departure.

Physical death is not the end, but the beginning. Physical death is merely a transition. It takes us out of this world, but we continue into eternity, into an existence with no end. Please stop and meditate on that. *No end!* Before sin, Adam and Eve lived in physical bodies that would never die. After their sin, and because of the transference of the sin nature through birth, everyone born since then lives in these physical bodies that grow old and one day die. With the exception of Christians alive at the moment the Rapture takes place, nobody escapes this moment of transition. When David was on his deathbed, he met with his son Solomon to share insights and instructions going forward. He told Solomon, *"I go the way of all the earth; be strong, therefore, and prove yourself a man"* (1 Kings 2:2). Joshua said the same thing to his leaders when he knew it was his time to die (Joshua 23:1-14).

Although to date, I've never been with someone at the point of their earthly departure, I've read many accounts from those who have. According to what they observe, when the child of God is dying and about to leave, they're described as peaceful, joyful, and full of excited anticipation as the glory of God opens the portals into heaven. On the other hand, the unsaved are described as fearful—even terrified, and full of dread as the dark doors of death close in around them.

As I said, I was saved at the age of 26. Even now, having served as my Lord's bondservant these many years, I shudder to think of how many times the Lord protected me from death. I've experienced more than one near fatal car crash, first as an 11-year-old boy, and later as a young adult in college and beyond. There were drug overdoses and drunk driving on multiple occasions. There was the willful and continual yielding to the lusts of the flesh. On and on I could go, but thanks be to God, His hand of protection was always there, even when I never knew it was. Thank God for parents who pray for wayward children! My Dad died in a single-car crash when I was 19 years old. He wasn't around as I struggled with sin in those confused and deceived days as a young man. Even so, I'm convinced it was the prayers of my caring Catholic mother, and many others I'm sure, that kept me from dying before I received my salvation. I cringe when I think of the many times I came to the precipice of death—coming so close to eternal destruction. One breath away. One car crash away. One drug overdose away. Thank

God for His loving hand that wouldn't let me go, until, like the prodigal son in Luke 15:17, I came to myself and got saved. And how did that happen? It happened because God orchestrated and arranged things in such a way that I was finally confronted with the true condition of my soul. We'll talk more about that later in this book.

This is the truth that no one can change or deny. One second after a person physically dies, they begin the journey to their eternal home. If Jesus was made Lord and Savior in life, they will go up to be with Him forever. If not, they will go down into the place of unspeakable suffering, surrounded by multitudes of other lost sinners and tormenting demons of all shapes and sizes. Whichever way they go, their destination is fixed. It will not change. They'll be where they are *forever*. Period.

CHAPTER 2

ONE QUESTION CHANGED MY LIFE

From September 1979 to May 1980, I was a first-year student at Rhema Bible Training College in Broken Arrow, Oklahoma, then known as Rhema Bible Training Center. Back then, our class schedule had classes starting at 8:30 a.m., and going until 12 noon, Monday through Friday. Each morning, after our first two morning classes, there was a 30-minute time block from 10:30 a.m. to 11:00 a.m., called *Share and Praise*. This was time allotted for any guest speakers, visiting missionaries, gospel singers, or any other notable Christian ministers or celebrities to speak to the student body, as they were led by the Holy Spirit.

Before *Share and Praise*, our classes were divided up between the first and second-year students. And because the number of first-year students was over 1,400, this group was further divided up into seven smaller groups. As a first year student, I was a member of group number three. But for *Share and Praise*, both first and second-year students were brought together in the main auditorium, and would remain seated together afterwards. At that point, Reverend Kenneth E. Hagin, our school's founder and president, would get up and teach the final class of the day. Those class sessions with him were such a wonderful time of teaching and instruction that I still glean from and apply in my ministry today.

One day, in the fall of 1979, Brother Hagin invited his good friend, Reverend Ernie Rebb to share whatever was on his heart to the student body during the *Share and Praise* time. When Brother Hagin introduced him as a good friend who was serving God as a missionary in the Philippines, I was immediately on the edge of my seat, because by that time I knew in my spirit the Lord was sending me to that country upon graduation the following year, in May 1980. I was eagerly anticipating whatever he would say that I could take and apply personally. As Brother Hagin sat down behind the pulpit, Brother Rebb got up and came to the podium. You could see he had his Bible and notes to refer to for his remarks to us. But what happened after that is something etched in my mind forever—words and actions that changed the direction of my life and ministry forever.

He stood there, looking at all of us. I was sitting about halfway back, in the seats to his right as he looked out over the student body, which that year numbered around 1,700 students—1,400 first-year and 300 second-year. He did a visual pan across the whole auditorium, from his right to his left. He did it slowly and purposefully. It took him several minutes to do this. He still had not said anything. Everyone, including me, was just looking back at him, wondering and watching. There was not a sound in that big room. Finally, he lowered his head and looked down at his Bible and prepared notes. It was obvious God was dealing with him about something. Because of the lights shining on his face up there on the platform, I could see there were tears coming down the right side of his cheeks. He then backed away from the pulpit for a few seconds, then briskly walked back to the pulpit and with his left hand gripping that side of the pulpit and his right hand raised in a clenched fist, he shouted out this one question across the auditorium:

"DO ANY OF YOU STUDENTS KNOW WHAT IT MEANS FOR A MAN TO PERISH?"

The entire building sat there in holy silence. There wasn't a sound. No one moved. Even as I recount this experience here to you, I still feel the heavy anointing as it was in that auditorium decades ago. When we talk and teach about a "rhema word from God," that was mine. The Greek word *rhema* means the "spoken Word of God." It means a truth stated in the Bible that permeates to the depths of the human spirit, an exploding personal revelation critical to a person's successful walk with the Lord.

I already knew that Romans 6:23 declared that the wages of sin is death. But the way this man said what he said, changed me. I don't remember a word he said after that. In that moment, God etched into my soul an awareness of heaven, hell, light, darkness—and the eternal consequences for rejecting the free gift of salvation. That one question has remained in my mind ever since, along with the reality of the duration of punishment that awaits a sinner upon physical death. I think about it almost every day. Every time I look at old pictures of people who have lived and died, I wonder where they are now, because they're still very much alive—in heaven or hell—forever.

Christian, do you really understand what it means for a man to perish without Jesus? Do you comprehend the level of pain and suffering they'll endure forever. Every time I cook food on our outdoor grill, I think about what it means for a man to perish. Every time I start a fire in our fireplace in the winter and tend to the fire throughout the evening, I think about what it means for a man to perish. What would it be like to descend into Hades (hell) upon death, to be tormented day and night by demons in untold ways of agony and pain, awaiting the Great White Throne Judgment of Revelation Chapter 20:12? There, standing before Almighty God, the books that chronicle all of your works are opened, and your daily decisions and words are examined against the Word of God (Matthew 12:37). Then the Book of Life is opened, and your name isn't in there. That means the consequences of your life of sin and rebellion means you're pronounced guilty as charged. You're then thrown into a lake of fire and brimstone with every other ungodly spirit, demon, or person that has ever lived—*and you are never getting out!* This is what it means for a man or woman to perish.

As you read this book at this very moment, millions upon millions of people are burning in fire and torment in the regions of the damned—what Jesus referred to as "the place of separation" when He took brother Sigmund into that horrible place. Use your imagination the way God gave it to be used. Picture people in heaven, the place of ultimate peace, bliss, joy, and happiness. They're in the presence of God, Jesus, the Holy Spirit, and every godly angel and righteous person that has ever lived. Wow! It's wonderful beyond comprehension.

In 2 Corinthians 12:1-4, we know the Apostle Paul had seen heaven in a vision, which is also why he said he wanted to depart and be with Christ, which was far better than staying here (Philippians 1:23). On the other hand, picture human beings bobbing in a lake of fire *forever*, surrounded by millions of other beings, with no hope of ever getting out. *That's what is at stake for every human being who dies without Christ. That's what it means for a man to perish.* No exceptions. No pardons. No parole board hearings. *Ever.* Do you understand this?

CHAPTER 3

PARTNERSHIP BY DIVINE CHOICE

With heaven and hell on the eternal horizon for every created creature, here's the amazing truth in this whole reality of life and death. Almighty God, the Lord Jesus and the Holy Spirit have chosen to limit their work of saving men from this horrible fate of damnation—to partnership with us! To me, that is just staggering! It's too awesome to comprehend. I can't wrap my mind around it—and neither can you. That's why we believers need to wake up, suck it up, and quit being a bunch of buttercups in these last days! It's time to get off the sidelines and get in the game. We don't need critics and complainers. We need participants and players.

Jesus commanded us to go into all the world to share the gospel with the lost (Mark 16:15-18). He did not tell us to sit around and wait for the world to come to us. We are being sent as heavenly emissaries in His name. We are His ambassadors, officially representing the Kingdom of Heaven to the world (2 Corinthians 5:20). He is trusting us to represent Him accurately to all the world. He is depending upon us to reach people everywhere with the truth (John 17:17). He loves them as much as He loves you and I—but *won't* impart to them eternal life until they ask for it. *And that doesn't happen without our participation.*

> *How then shall they call on Him in whom they have not believed? And how shall they believe in Him of whom they have not heard? And how shall they hear without a preacher? And how shall they preach unless they are sent? As it is written: "How beautiful are the feet of those who preach the gospel of peace,* **Who bring glad tidings of good things!***"*
>
> —Romans 10:14-15

SUCH A LEVEL OF LOVE

> *Fulfill my joy by being like-minded,* **having the same love,** *being of one accord of one mind. Let nothing be done through selfish ambition or conceit, but in lowliness of mind let each esteem others better than himself.* **Let each of you look out not only for his own interests, but also for the interests of others.** *Let this mind be in you which was also in Christ Jesus, who, being in the form of God, did not consider it robbery to be equal with God, but made Himself of no reputation, taking the form of a bondservant, and coming in the likeness of men. And being found in appearance as a man, He humbled Himself and became obedient to the point of death, even the death of the cross.*
>
> —Philippians 2:2-8

Look at all that Jesus did to make it possible for people to be saved. There is absolutely nothing that can compare to the degree of love the Father, Son, and Holy Spirit demonstrated to carry out the plan of salvation. Imagine—the Second Person of the Trinity—the Creator of all things that includes us, left heaven and by the power of the Holy Spirit, took upon Himself a human body for the express purpose of fulfilling the righteous requirements that were demanded by a just and holy God. For more than 33 years, Jesus lived on Earth and lived a spotless life that completed the task that no other man could ever accomplish. He fulfilled the law and made our salvation possible.

But at what price? The price of voluntary submission to the horrific level of suffering the Word of God reveals. Through the secular and religious puppets of hell, our Lord had to endure the fury of Satan himself. He was tortured without mercy. He had his beard ripped out of His face. He was repeatedly slapped while blindfolded. Long, pointed thorns were somehow fashioned into a "crown," then jammed into His skull. His back was whipped and beaten so badly nothing was left but raw, bleeding muscle tissue.

According to T.J. McCrossan's book, *Bodily Healing and the Atonement*, the word "stripes" found in 1 Peter 2:24 is actually in the singular tense, not plural. That means His back was whipped to the point where there was no flesh left. His entire back was nothing but exposed muscle, bone, and sinew. No skin left to see. Just one big stripe, not many. Usually, when victims were whipped like this, they never lived to reach whip (stripe) number 39. But according to McCrossan's research in his book, he says that if the Jews were administering the whipping, the law would require them to stop at stripe 39—however, the Romans had no such restrictions.

That means because of their animosity toward the Jews in general, they could just go on and on with the whipping to their heart's content, which is more than likely what they did with Jesus. Either way, by the time a victim was hit with 39 or more whip stripes, they were dead from pain, blunt force trauma, blood loss, and shock. Jesus had to endure all of this, and then be forced to carry his own heavy cross uphill to the place where He was to die. And how was He put up on the cross? With heavy, jagged nails pounded right through His hands and feet. When this was done to those being crucified, you could hear their screaming for miles, but Jesus never opened His mouth (Isaiah 53:7). Incredible!

After all of that agony, He was made to be sin for us while up on that cross, forsaken by God to die as our substitute and pay for the sins we've committed (Matthew 27:46). That meant suffering for three days and nights in hell (Hades), the place of separation, where sinners go in the afterlife. There He continued to suffer under the wrath of a pure and holy God, serving the penalty for what we as sinners have done, and what we as sinners rightfully deserved (Isaiah Chapter 53). Are you getting the big picture here? God—the Creator of the universe and everything in it—allowed Himself to be treated in this way and to suffer in this way, all because He loves us more than we can ever comprehend. It's a level of love that we'll never be able to fathom or understand. It just drives us to our knees in worship, praise, and adoration.

GOD'S PLAN INCLUDES OUR PART

Jesus won't save anyone—those He loves this much—unless we participate in the plan! All of the work He did has set the stage for you and me to go into all the world to tell the world what happened, and why. This started with the 3,000 souls Peter led to the Lord for salvation on the day of Pentecost (Acts 2:41), and will continue until the Lord returns, as promised (Acts 1:11).

Years ago, when Ethel and I first started out and had a place of our own, we bought a very nice Christmas nativity scene, complete with the usual figurines that represent the key players regarding the birth of Christ. Each Christmas, that manger would be taken out of storage, and included with all the other traditional ornaments and decorations we Christians like to adorn our homes with. But the more I meditated on the sheer magnitude of what it means to be an ambassador for the Lord entrusted with His gospel, I decided to leave that Nativity scene out on the mantle all year round, in a place where anyone can see it readily every day—especially me. Why? Because I want to be visually reminded of how much God loved the world, exactly as Jesus pointed out to Nicodemus in John 3:1-21. And every day, in my personal devotions before the Lord, I look over at that Nativity scene, and with hands raised high, praise the Lord God for loving me so much He would come from heaven like He did to do what He did.

> **What shall I render to the Lord** for all His benefits toward me?
>
> —Psalms 116:12

How can we ever repay God for all of his goodness, kindness, and mercy which He bestows upon us every single day? How can we give back to Him anything that shows Him we understand that we are what we are solely because of His grace (1 Corinthains 15:10)? There's really only one way it can be done, and that can be summed up in three words: *responsibility, availability, and accountability.*

RESPONSIBILITY

> *To me, who am less than the least of all the saints, this grace was given,* **that I should preach among the Gentiles the unsearchable riches of Christ.**
>
> —Ephesians 3:8

> *But* **when it pleased God**, *who separated me from my mother's womb and called me through His grace, to reveal*

> *His Son in me,* **that I might preach Him among the Gentiles,** *I did not immediately confer with flesh and blood.*
>
> —Galatians 1:15-16

AVAILABILTY

> *Also I heard the voice of the Lord, saying: "Whom shall I send, and who will go for Us?" Then I said,* **"Here am I! Send me."**
>
> —Isaiah 6:8

ACCOUNTABILITY

> *You did not choose Me, but* **I chose you and appointed you that you should go and bear fruit, and that your fruit should remain**, *that whatever you ask the father in My name He may give you.*
>
> —John 15:16

> *For if I preach the gospel, I have nothing to boast of, for necessity is laid upon me; yes,* **woe is me** *if I do not preach the gospel!*
>
> —1 Corinthians 9:16

The responsibility that goes with being entrusted with the gospel is great. Therefore, our availability to the Great Commission must be more important than anything else. This is the most important choice any believer will make. Because whether we obey the call or not, we'll be held accountable to God for the life we lived, and the choices we made. Be a wise believer and never forget this truth: *the top priority is to keep the top priority the top priority.*

CHAPTER 4

ETERNAL DESTINATIONS

*Go into all the world and preach the gospel to every creature. He who believes and is baptized **will be saved**; but he who does not believe **will be condemned**.*

—Mark 16:15-16

God is not willing for anyone to perish, but to have everyone repent and receive His free gift of salvation (2 Peter 3:9). But sad to say, most people who have lived and died made the choice to reject God's offer, and are now suffering in Hades, which is the present place of torment, awaiting their final sentencing at the Great White Throne Judgment (Revelation 20:11-14).

When a person leaves their body at the moment of physical death, they either go up or down, depending on the choices they've made and the words they've spoken (Deuteronomy 30:19 /Matthew 12:37). Whichever way they go, they go for *forever*. This is the reality for everyone born into this earth. We are all spirits with souls, living in physical bodies. Spirits and souls are eternal—they can never cease to exist. They can't be killed. They can't die in the same sense as our physical bodies die. A story Jesus told while here on Earth illustrates the astonishing truth of this.

> "There was a certain rich man who was clothed in purple and fine linen and fared sumptuously every day. But there was a certain beggar named Lazarus, full of sores, who was laid at his gate, desiring to be fed with the crumbs which fell from the rich man's table. Moreover the dogs came and licked his sores. So it was that the beggar died, and was carried by the angels to Abraham's bosom. The rich man also died and was buried. And being in torment in Hades, he lifted up his eyes and saw Abraham afar off, and Lazarus in his bosom. Then he cried and said, 'Father Abraham, have mercy on me, and send Lazarus that he may dip the tip of his finger in water and cool my tongue; for I am tormented in this flame.' But Abraham said, 'Son, remember that in your lifetime you received your good things, and likewise Lazarus evil things; but now he is comforted and you are tormented. And besides all this, between us and you there is a great gulf fixed, so that those who want to pass from here to you cannot, nor can those from there pass to us.' Then he said, 'I beg you therefore, father, that you would send him to my father's house, for I have five brothers, that he may testify to them, lest they also come to this place of torment.' Abraham said to him, 'They have Moses and the prophets; let them hear them.' And he said, 'No, father Abraham; but if one goes to them from the dead, they will repent.' But he said to him, **'If they do not hear Moses and the prophets, neither will they be persuaded though one rise from the dead.'"**
>
> —Luke 16:19-31

ETERNAL DESTINATIONS

This is not a parable. It's a true story. Nowhere does it say, "and Jesus spoke this parable unto them," or "the kingdom of God is likened unto . . ." There really was a rich man who lived on earth, and there really was a poor, sick man laid at his front gate. The recounting of this story tells us where both men went when they died. Good for Lazarus, but terrible for the rich man. The poor beggar isn't poor or sick anymore. When He died, he was carried by angels into Abraham's Bosom, where he waited for Jesus to come and carry out the plan of salvation. He is now in heaven, along with every other person who has lived and made the choice to follow the Word of God and be born again.

But the rich man, when he died, he didn't just lose all his earthly wealth—he lost the ability to receive God's free gift of salvation by faith. Jesus took Lazarus to heaven, when he led all the Old Testament saints out from Abraham's Bosom and into heaven (Ephesians 4:8). But the rich man is still right where he was on the day he died, thousands of years ago. He's still in Hades, still suffering in pain and anguish. He's still crying out for someone to dip their finger in water and touch his tongue, so that just for a moment, he might find relief from the pain of the flames in that place. *He's still waiting.* Waiting for someone who will *never* come, waiting for something that will *never* happen. Every unbeliever who dies lost is in the same boat as the rich man in hell. Their present is pain, suffering, and torment. Their future is their sentencing at the Great White Judgment. Their eternity is banishment into a lake of fire and brimstone. The horror of this is too overwhelming to contemplate, but contemplate it we must, because that's reality.

> *Then He spoke a parable to them, saying: "The ground of a certain rich man yielded plentifully. And he thought within himself, saying, 'What shall I do, since I have no room to store my crops?' So he said, 'I will do this: I will pull down my barns and build greater, and there I will store all my crops and all my*

goods. And I will say to my soul, "Soul, you have many goods laid up for many years; take your ease; eat, drink, and be merry."' But God said to him, 'Fool! This night your soul will be required of you; then whose will those things be which you have provided. **So is he who lays up treasure for himself, and is not rich towards God.'"**

—Luke 12:16-21

This parable is being lived out by millions of people around the world today, including many Christians. Ralph Mahoney, a godly, missions-minded man who is now in heaven, founded a ministry called World Map https://www.world-map.com. He once made a statement I've never forgotten. He said: *I pray for the day when Christians are as willing to invest in the business of winning souls as much as they are willing to acquire and enjoy possessions for themselves.*

I pray the same prayer consistently. In my ministry travels for the Lord, I see brethren everywhere—rich and poor alike—who are living selfish, self-centered lives, without a care in the world for the lost all around them. Multitudes of Christians have been blinded to the reality of the unseen world and the finality of our eternal abode. I consider this to be one of the greatest, if not *the* greatest, tragedy on earth today. Why? Because we are the only ones designated by God to share the truth with the world. Think about that!

In every way possible, the devil wants to hide, minimize, and cover up what happens to a person once they die without Christ. One second after death, as they begin to descend into hell, every lost person on earth will begin screaming out for mercy, willing to repent and accept Jesus as Lord and Savior, but by then it's too late. Judgment is final and eternal.

ETERNAL DESTINATIONS

THE REALITY OF ETERNITY

God is my witness. I think about this eternity every day. Especially when I see the people all around me, busy and entangled with the affairs of this life (2 Timothy 2:1-7). This applies to believers as well as unbelievers.

> For the **love of money** is a root of all kinds of evil, for which some have strayed from the faith in their greediness, and pierced themselves though with many sorrows.
> —1 Timothy 6:10

It's bad enough when we see sinners driven by nothing more than the love of money, but it's especially tragic when we see believers doing the same. Notice that Paul warned Timothy expressly about this dangerous temptation and trap. As it is today, so it was back then. Some *strayed from the faith* in Bible times, and many believers have done the same today.

> The proud have hidden a **snare** for me, and **cords**; they have spread a **net** by the wayside; they have set **traps** for me.
> —Psalms 140:5

The devil uses many tools and tactics to bring down a Christian. Here we see four of them. There are *snares, cords, nets, and traps*. Each of these represents a particular way the devil tries to influence our decisions, keeping us away from a life with clear focus on the reality of eternity. He doesn't care how he convinces us to selfishly hoard our resources—just so we do! Always keep an eye out for "opportunities" that could break you financially and prevent you from being an active player in world evangelism. Many believers have been tripped up with demonic snares, cords, nets, or traps. Don't let that be you!

When it comes to money, we must always see it for what it is—and isn't. It's not a god to be worshipped, even though the devil tries to convince us otherwise. It's just a tool to be used for God's glory. Even though money is something physical and tangible, it has the ability to be used to impact lives spiritually all around the world. That is amazing. From God's viewpoint, money is to be used for two things in life. First, money is to be used to pay for the cost of living. Groceries, utilities, vehicles, mortgages, education, and all the rest—what we call paying our bills and putting food on the table! Second, money is to be used to honor God as our sole source of provision, funding the Great Commissions of Mark 16:15-18, and Matthew 28:18-20. That's what tithing, giving offerings, and giving to the poor is all about—operating the laws of spiritual prosperity found in the Bible.

That's why, once we have our bills paid and we're not spending our remaining cash reserves frivolously, I exhort Christians to be generous with God, and put Him first when it comes to making "wise investments" with their time, talent, and money. Giving towards God's work—especially to missions—is a sure-fired recipe for success, in this life as well as in the next. Unlike any investment in the world's system of finance, there is no risk whatsoever. God's Word guarantees a massive ROI, which is what the world refers to as our "Return on Investment" (Mark 10:29-30). Yet, we see multitudes of Christians who don't tithe or give above their tithe, while prioritizing their personal acquisitions selfishly. How sad to watch Christians do this over and over again. No matter how much we spend to make ourselves more comfortable with the latest and greatest "thing" today, it's eventually going to be replaced by a newer "thing" tomorrow (Colossians 2:22). I shake my head and shudder because of what I know, and what the Bible warns every one of us about.

There are billions of people living today with a very cavalier attitude toward life on the outside, while simultaneously suppressing their fear of death on the inside (Hebrews 2:15). People talk about making a "bucket list" of things to do before they die, but that's nothing more than an attempt to manage their fear of death itself. Jesus overcame that fear, but it takes faith to believe that and tap into the freedom that only He can provide. People can work to check all the boxes on their bucket list, but in the end, it's all just a lot of smoke and mirrors. You can go where you want, do what you want, and have the time of your life, but someday death will come knocking on the door, and there's nothing anyone can do about that. The only bucket list that means anything at all is one that focuses on finding and fulfilling God's perfect will for our lives. So far, I've never seen or heard of any sinner's bucket list that was comprised of doing more things for Jesus.

Personally, I constantly thank God that He protected me from killing myself when I was young, dumb, and unsaved, with all the stupid and reckless things I said, did, and got involved with before I was saved at age 26. Hell is full of people who were just like me back then, but now they're in that place of pain and torment, and will *never get out*. In my life, there were many opportunities for death to snatch me away to an eternity of torment. But God . . . ! But God . . . ! Thank God Almighty I'm not where so many are now, lost forever in flames, awaiting their judgment and sentencing to a lake of fire and brimstone (Revelation 20:11-15).

THE BICYCLE RIDER

The Holy Spirit reminds me of a tragic story involving a young bicyclist in Tucson, Arizona, which is where our worldwide ministry is based. Every year in November, on the Saturday before the Thanksgiving holiday, the city holds a bicycle race called El Tour de Tucson. It's famous and draws competitors from many nations. Thousands of bicyclists of all ages and skill levels compete. There are three options for a competitor to choose from when participating in this race, with varying lengths and degree of physical fitness for each.

There is the main racecourse of between 100 and 110 miles. There is an intermediate racecourse with a distance of around sixty-five miles, and a short course of about thirty miles for beginners. I rode the main racecourse for three consecutive years, from 2005 to 2007, when I was younger and had more time to train for such an event. I was able to finish in just under 7 hours each time. Every year, as the race date approaches, there are groups of bicyclists riding all over the city, training for the event.

I read an article in the local newspaper about one such rider who was tragically killed while training for the El Tour de Tucson. He was doing what we call "wind sprints," which is an exercise designed to develop aerobic lung capacity for short, powerful bursts of speed. To do this, a bicyclist lowers their head, drops down into a crouched position on the bike, and pedals as hard as possible for 1 or 2 minutes, then rests for 1 or 2 minutes, then repeats the process several times. Doing the wind sprints with his head down and not looking where he was going, this bicyclist plowed into the back of a parked car at full speed. The collision snapped his neck, and he died on the spot.

He was a young man in his early twenties, and whatever the condition of his spirit was at the time of the crash has determined where he will spend eternity. I hope he was a born again child of God. If so, he's with Jesus in heaven forever. That's the good news of the gospel. If not, he's in hell today, with no hope of ever getting out. Just like that. He woke up that day as a young man, physically fit with his whole life in front of him, training to ride and compete in this race. I'm sure he had goals and objectives he had established for his life. A college degree and an excellent job afterwards. Getting married and having a family. Saving money for the upcoming expenses of life. All of that gone in an unexpected instant. Forever redeemed or forever lost. That's the consequence for waiting until it was too late. Just like the parable Jesus taught about the rich man building bigger barns to hold all of his worldly increase.

THE NEARBY NEIGHBOR

Another example deals with a neighbor of ours in Tucson, Arizona, who lived just a few doors down from us. I would see him frequently in his truck driving by, while I was taking early morning prayer walks around the neighborhood. He would nod in recognition as I waved while he passed by, but I never knew his name and never really got to know him personally.

One day I met another one of my neighbors out at the mailbox, when I went out to get my mail. She was walking her dog, and we stopped for some friendly conversation. Her name is Carol, and as we stood there talking, she asked me if I had heard about what happened to "Glen." I said no, and when I said I didn't know who that was, she proceeded to let me know it was this same neighbor that I had been waving at in the mornings. She also told me that Glen and her husband were avid private pilots, who each flew their own hand-built single-engine aircraft they kept in an airport hangar at a nearby regional airport. Carol went on to tell me that just a few days before, the two men were flying to a small town called Eloy for lunch, about 50 miles to the northwest of Tucson. On the way back home, Glen's plane malfunctioned somehow, and he was killed when his airplane crashed and burned. When she told me about it, I went online to see if there was anything I could find about what happened. And sure enough, on the evening news, there were videos taken from news helicopters that had been hovering over the crash site. The impact was so severe, and the ensuing flames so intense, that there was nothing left to see of aircraft wreckage. All you could see was a small patch of scorched earth where the plane had hit the ground, with police cars and fire trucks all around the black patch of earth.

I've thought about this many times since, probably because I knew this man in a more personal way. I don't know if Glen is in heaven or hell today, but the accident itself reminds me of the fragility of life, and how people are unwittingly just an unexpected accident away from eternity. People wake up in the morning, expecting their day to be like any other, and before the sun goes down, they're either in heaven or hell—forever. They didn't expect it or plan on it, but it happened anyway. Death is an enemy that is forever crouching at our doorstep. In a split second of time, people can find themselves leaving their physical bodies and either ascending or descending. And like I said before—whichever way they're going, they're going *forever*. I honestly don't think most Christians have really taken time to wrap their minds around the reality of eternity. All the more reason for me to sound the alarm over and over! Why? Because I've been entrusted with the gospel of Jesus Christ, that's why.

THE GREATEST TORMENT

The greatest torment for those lost in the flames of fire is their memory of life on earth, and the many times their words sealed their fate in hell. Abraham said to the rich man, *"Son, remember...."* In heaven or hell, the human spirit has all the faculties they had while living in their physical bodies. All their senses are still there, magnified much more than they were in this life—including memory. Why do you think the Holy Spirit inspired Luke to include this story in his gospel? Why do you think these warnings appear over and over in Scripture—Old Testament as well as New Testament? Because God so loved the world He gave Jesus, that whoever believes in Him *shall not perish, but have everlasting life* (John 3:16).

ETERNAL DESTINATIONS

*The Lord is not slack concerning His promise, as some count slackness, but is longsuffering toward us, **not willing that any should perish** but that all should come to repentance.*

—2 Peter 3:9

*Therefore you, O son of man, say to the house of Israel: 'Thus you say, "If our transgressions and our sins lie upon us, and we pine away in them, how can we then live?"' Say to them: 'As I live,' says the Lord God, **'I have no pleasure in the death of the wicked**, but that the wicked turn from his way and live. Turn, turn from your evil ways: For why should you die, O house of Israel?'*

—Ezekiel 33:10-11

*Moreover He said to me: "Son of man, receive into your heart all My words that I speak to you, and hear with your ears. And go, get to the captives, to the children of your people, and **speak to them and tell them**, 'Thus says the Lord God,' whether they hear, or whether they refuse."*

—Ezekiel 3:10-11

*Now it came to pass at the end of seven days that the word of the Lord came to me, saying, "Son of man, I have made you a watchman for the house of Israel; therefore **hear a word from My mouth, and give them warning from Me**: When I say to the wicked, 'You shall surely die,' and you give him no warning, nor speak to warn the wicked from his wicked way, to save his life, that same wicked man shall die in his iniquity; but his blood I will require at your hand. Yet, if you warn the wicked, and he does not turn from his wickedness, nor from* *his wicked way, he shall die in his iniquity; but you have delivered your soul."*

—Ezekiel 3:16-19

*Him we preach, **warning every man** and teaching every man in all wisdom, that we may present every man perfect in Christ Jesus. To this end I also labor, striving according to His working which works in me mightily.*

—Colossians 1:28-29

Every Christian is a watchman. Our job is to preach, teach, and warn people about the reality of eternity. People are one car crash away, one heart attack away, one stroke away, one tragic accident away from an eternity lost in hell. We're not the Savior. We're just the messengers. We do what we can, and God will do what we can't. We can't save anyone, but we can warn them, *and woe to us if we don't, because we've been entrusted with the gospel.*

PART TWO:

THE RESPONSIBILITY

CHAPTER 5

ENTRUSTED WITH THE GOSPEL

*But as we have been approved by God to be **entrusted with the gospel**, even so we speak, not as pleasing men, but God who tests our hearts.*

—1 Thessalonians 2:4

By virtue of the new birth, every Christian is approved by God to represent Him to the world. That means every Christian has been entrusted with the gospel. This is the greatest honor any man or woman can be given in life. Nothing else can compare. The Word of God is the only source of accurate information leading to eternal life. By God's choice, we're commanded to go into all the world to preach it, teach it, and warn people about the consequences for rejecting it (Colossians 1:28-29; 1 Corinthians 4:14). God has entrusted us with the *one and only message* that can forever reverse the path each sinner is on. Whoever rejects that message—the gospel—will suffer the eternal consequences for such a decision.

Entrusted for Eternity

> *Go into all the world and **preach the gospel** to every creature. He who believes and is baptized will be saved; but he who does not believe will be condemned.*
>
> —Mark 16:15-16

> *"All authority has been given to Me in heaven and on earth. Go therefore and make disciples of all the nations, baptizing them in the name of the Father and of the Son and of the Holy Spirit, **teaching them** to observe all things that I have commanded you; and lo, I am with you always, even to the end of the age." Amen.*
>
> —Matthew 28:18-20

We've been told to do something with this gospel that goes beyond what it did for us personally. We've been told to live a life that measures up to the task at hand. We've been told that if we don't get involved in spirit, soul, and body, lives will be lost forever, suffering eternally without end. Read Ezekiel Chapters 3 and 33. Those chapters describe the situation as it is on earth today, and what happens when the people of God fail to discharge their responsibilities to warn unbelievers of the consequences of rejecting the gospel.

If the sinners are warned and still choose to reject the gospel, their blood is on their own head. But if we—who are described as God's "watchmen"—disobey God and fail to give sinners the warning, the sinner will die and go to hell, *but their blood will be on our hands.* I have no idea what that means, but it can't be good! In short, we were entrusted to share the gospel, and we didn't do it. God entrusted us with the message to share, and we violated that trust by refusing to preach, teach, and warn people. Why? Because we didn't grasp the eternal significance of being entrusted with the gospel. This is one of the greatest tragedies on earth.

APPROVED BY GOD

It's very important to know that Christians are already approved *by God* to be entrusted with the gospel. That means any born again believer, from the moment of the new birth, is able to represent Jesus to the world, and authorized to do so in His Name. That includes you. We don't have to go to someone's Bible school to become approved by men—we're already approved by God! That's why Paul goes on to say that pleasing men is completely unnecessary. We work to please God, and after that, it doesn't matter who "approves" or "disapproves" of us. None of those believers in Thessalonica were polished Bible school graduates. None of them had titles in front and initials behind their name. No, sir! These people were just ordinary saints who had the Holy Spirit dwelling inside of them. That fact made them approved by God to represent all of heaven to the whole world down here. Nothing else was necessary.

Now of course, we're also told to study to show ourselves approved by God (2 Timothy 2:15). But those instructions don't have to be completed before anyone can go out there and share Jesus with others. After all, no matter how much "studying" we do, and how much knowledge we "acquire," our sum total of knowledge on all things pertaining to God is miniscule at best. In other words, we'll all be learning about the things of God forever—we'll never reach a point where we know everything! Yes, we should study to show ourselves approved by God, but never forget the fact that the knowledge we have about God's plan of redemption is worthless to the sinner until we realize we're entrusted to take what we know (however little it may be quantitively), and share it with those who need to know what we know.

That's why even baby Christians can witness effectively for Jesus, because one of the best ways to "witness" is to simply share your personal testimony. What God does for us personally is our most powerful witnessing tool because nobody can contest it. We know it happened because it happened to us, and God is no respecter of persons (Acts 10:34)! So we can tell people that what He did for us is what He'll do for them. Share that! Talk about that! As we grow in knowledge through Bible study, there will be more and more verses we can use when witnessing, but in the beginning, just tell people that the same Jesus who delivered you is the same Jesus who wants to deliver them. Simple!

PLEASING GOD IS ALL THAT MATTERS

> *But when you do a charitable deed, do not let your left hand know what your right hand is doing, that your charitable deed may be in secret; and your Father who sees in secret will Himself* **reward you openly**.
>
> —Matthew 6:3-4

Being entrusted with the gospel is a responsibility we have before the Lord, and to no one else. If God is pleased with what we do in the Name of Jesus, who cares if anyone else likes it or not? I mean, really? What difference does anyone else's opinion make when we do what we do because we're told to by the Lord? As it says in Romans 14:4, who are we to judge another man's servant? To his own master he stands or falls. This is what Paul told the Corinthians when some of them came against him and his ministry, and what he told the Galatians as well.

> *Let a man so consider us, as servants of Christ and stewards of the mysteries of God. Moreover it is required in stewards that one be found faithful. But with me it is a very small thing that I should be judged by you or by a human court. In fact, I do not even judge myself. For I know of nothing against myself, yet I am not justified by this;* **but he who judges me is the Lord**.
>
> —1 Corinthians 4:1-4

ENTRUSTED WITH THE GOSPEL

*For do I now persuade men, **or God**? Or do I seek to please men? For if I still pleased men, I would not be a **bondservant** of Christ.*

—Galatians 1:10

What does the Bible tell us in Romans, Chapter 8:31-39? The next time you feel the pressure to bow down to the opinions of men, read that Bible passage slowly and prayerfully. Among other wonderful truths, those verses tell us that if God be for us, who can be against us (vs 31)? They also remind us that God is our judge, and His opinion is the only one that matters (vs 33). Keep these things in mind, the next time you're tempted to alter your conversation or your actions because of what others are saying about you.

Listen! We can never please everybody all the time, so don't bother trying. Indeed, that's *mission impossible!* Seek to please the Lord, and let that be your one and only measurement regarding success or failure in this life. James 2:12 says it this way: *So speak and so do, as those who will be judged by the law of liberty.* That's enough. God is our judge, and His law of liberty is His criteria for our judgment. The law of liberty is the law of agape love in the New Testament. Love does no harm to others; therefore agape love is the fulfillment of the Old Testament law (Romans 13:10). When I stand before Jesus on the day of my judgment, I want Him to say to me, "Well done, good and faithful servant!" (Matthew 25:21,23) I'm sure you want Him to say the same thing to you. In this life, our one and only benchmark for success as a Christian is this right here. Is God pleased with our lives, or not?

Jesus Himself set the bar for all of us. More than once, God the Father audibly broke through the heavens to let people know how pleased He was with His Son Jesus.

*And suddenly a voice came from heaven, saying, "This is My beloved son, in whom **I am well pleased."***

—Matthew 3:17

*While he was still speaking, behold, a bright cloud overshadowed them; and suddenly a voice came out of the cloud, saying, "This is My beloved Son, in whom **I am well pleased. Hear Him!"***

—Matthew 17:5

How do we live our lives like Jesus lived His? By finding out what God wants us to say and do, and then saying or doing it. How people respond should have no bearing upon the situation at that moment.

*For I have not spoken on My own authority; but the Father who sent Me gave Me a command, **what I should say and what I should speak.***

—John 12:49

*"I can of myself do nothing. As I hear, I judge; and My judgment is righteous, because I do not seek My own will **but the will of the Father who sent me.***

—John 5:30

When we say and do what the Lord commands us to say and do, we're going to make some people very happy, and some people very angry. So be it. We're not down here to follow Dale Carnegie's course on *How to Win Friends & Influence People*. We're down here to obey God. Period. Using the Lord Jesus as our example once again, the Bible records the good, the bad, and the ugly exchanges between our Lord and the Jews. Numerous heated exchanges took place. As an example, after listening to His first public sermon in His own hometown, people weren't exactly lining up to buy His books and get on His mailing list! Simply by telling them who He was and what He was here to do, He got His neighbors so riled up, they tried to drag Him over to a nearby cliff and throw Him off (Luke 4:28-29). Even when His Bible studies started off well, by the time He was finished teaching, some of His own staff walked away, shaking their heads in disillusionment and confusion.

> *Therefore many of His disciples, when they heard this, said, "This is a hard saying, who can understand it?" When Jesus knew in Himself that His disciples **complained** about this, He said to them, "Does this offend you? From that time **many** of His disciples **went back and walked with Him no more**. Then Jesus said to the twelve, "Do you also want to go away?"*
>
> —John 6:60-61,66-67

So, make up your mind. Are you going to cave in under the pressure of public opinion? Or are you going to prove yourself faithful to the Lord, and be a dependable and accurate mouthpiece for the kingdom of heaven?

> *You therefore, my son, **be strong in the grace** that is in Christ Jesus. And the things that you have heard from me among many witnesses, commit these to faithful men who will be able to teach others also.*
>
> —2 Timothy 2:1-2

> *Consider now, for the Lord has chosen you to build a house for the sanctuary; **be strong, and do it**.*
>
> —1 Chronicles 28:10

We are told to tell the truth. This is what the world needs to hear, and we are the only ones ordained by God to deliver the goods. Period.

CHAPTER 6

ENTRUSTED WITH A STEWARDSHIP

*For if I preach the gospel, I have nothing to boast of, for necessity is laid upon me; yes, woe is me if I do not preach the gospel. For if I do this willingly, I have a reward; but if against my will, **I have been entrusted with a stewardship**. What is my reward then? That when I preach the gospel, I may present the gospel of Christ without charge, that I may not abuse my authority in the gospel.*

—1 Corinthians 9:16-18

*Blessed be the God and Father of our Lord Jesus Christ, the Father of mercies and God of all comfort, who comforts us in all our tribulation, that **we may be able to comfort those who are in any trouble**, with the comfort with which we ourselves are comforted by God. For we do not want you to be ignorant, brethren, of our trouble which came to us in Asia:*

that we were burdened beyond measure, above strength, so that we despaired even of life.

—1 Corinthians 1:3-5,8

No matter how we feel on any given day, we're *still* entrusted with the truth that sets men free (John 8:31-32). In reading Paul's letters to the different churches, there were many times when he went and did what God told him to do, even though he suffered terribly for doing so. Read Chapters 1, 4, 6, and 11 from 2 Corinthains, and try to imagine the level of pain and persecution he endured. One time he complained about the thorn in his flesh from Satan, but God just reminded him that His grace was sufficient for what he was told to do (2 Corinthians 12:7). So, he just "sucked it up," as we say, and went on doing what he knew had to be done. I'm sure when Jesus Himself was in the Garden of Gethsemane, sweating as it were great drops of blood, pleading with His Father to give Him an out, He didn't feel like going through the horrible experience of the cross. But because He knew He was entrusted with the responsibility—the stewardship—to do what had to be done to give all men the chance for eternal salvation, He did what had to be done. This is how He conquered the temptation of the moment by saying *"Nevertheless, not My will, but Your will be done."*

NECESSITY IS LAID UPON US

I've been there in ministry many times—and perhaps you have, too. We might be exhausted physically. We might be battling sickness or disease. We might be emotionally compromised. We might be going through terrible degrees of persecution. We might be going through all of the above, and more. But because we're entrusted with the gospel, we *decide* to remain available in whatever ways the Lord needs us. Regardless of the adverse circumstances around us, we know necessity is laid upon us, and we will be held accountable to God for how we responded to Him—saying or doing whatever the situation requires in the name of Jesus (Isaiah 6:8). No exceptions and no excuses. And here's our eternal hope: payday *will* eventually come. If we share Jesus with the right heart in obedience to the Holy Spirit's leading, we get rewards someday in heaven that we'll have and enjoy forever.

> *And whatever you do, **do it heartily**, as to the Lord and not to men, knowing that from the Lord **you will receive the reward** of the inheritance; for you serve the Lord Christ.*
>
> —Colossians 3:23

On the other side of that coin, if we do what the Lord asks us to do with the wrong attitude, we cheat ourselves out of the rewards set aside in heaven for us. One way or the other, we're still responsible to God for completing our particular assignments. We're still commanded to follow orders no matter how we feel about it. In the military, soldiers do what they're commanded to do whether they like it or not. Jesus is our Commander-in-Chief, and He has entrusted us with the only message that can save a soul from hell. That being so, He expects us to understand the gravity of the situation for every person we're put in contact with. We don't know the future for people like God does. If He's entrusting us with His Word, His message, and His love for the people, we must present the truth enthusiastically, without apology or hesitation. That's divine stewardship in action. It's important to remember that God knows the future for everyone. We don't. For all we know, we might be the last opportunity a person has to hear the gospel before death arrives at their doorstep.

SPIRITUAL UNDERSTANDING

In short, we're entrusted to see the "bigger picture." We're entrusted to know and understand the reality of the two worlds every person is a part of. We're entrusted to understand the spirit world is the parent world, and all laws in this world are subject to the laws of that world. We're entrusted to understand we are eternal spirits that possess a soul, living in physical bodies. We're entrusted to understand that physical death removes the power of choice, and the choices made in this life seal our eternal dwelling place. We're entrusted to understand that as Christians, the words we speak and the lives we live are the *only* ways we represent Jesus as His ambassadors (James 2:12). And finally, we're entrusted to understand we have been given authority from Jesus to operate in His name, and do His business until He comes (Luke 19:13). We do that the same way Paul did it.

> Him we preach, warning **every man** and teaching **every man** in all wisdom that we may present **every man** perfect in Christ Jesus.
>
> —Colossians 1:28

Who do we preach, teach, and warn? *Every man!* We deliver the full gospel, not a partial gospel. We give the truth without prejudice, giving everyone the options to choose life or death, heaven or hell, *forever* (Deuteronomy 30:19).

> So Cornelius said, "Four days ago I was fasting until this hour, and at the ninth hour I prayed in my house, and behold, a man stood before me in bright clothing, and said, 'Cornelius, your prayer has been heard, and your alms are remembered in the sight of God. Send therefore to Joppa and call Simon here, whose surname is Peter. He is lodging in the house of Simon, a tanner, by the sea. **When he comes, he will speak**

to you.' *So I sent to you immediately, and you have done well to come. Now therefore,* **we are all present before God, to hear all the things commanded you by God.***"*

—Acts 10:30-33

When I read about Peter's encounter with Cornelious and his household, I try to envision the scene from heaven's perspective. All these people, including Cornelius himself, are all assembled to hear words from a man they've never met or known before. No doubt, they're talking amongst themselves, wondering why it's so important that their master has called this meeting and required everyone to be present. Cornelius rehearses what he experienced four days earlier, trying to help his household understand the importance of this gathering. So, here they are, a group of people that God loves and for whom Jesus gave His life, waiting patiently for four days.

PEOPLE ARE WAITING FOR YOU

What are they waiting for? Waiting to hear all things Peter has been commanded by God to share. Waiting to hear from a man who has been entrusted with the gospel. They really don't know what to expect, but God does. I can see the room in my mind. Full of people who are about to have their eternal destiny changed from death to life, from the power of Satan to the power of God. All because one man was available, knowing that obedience is not an option for the entrusted, especially when it takes blind faith to go and say what needs to be said to people who are ready to hear. Peter had no idea there were a bunch of Gentiles in a far-away city ready to receive Jesus as Lord and Savior, but the Lord did. So the Holy Spirit springs into action to make this meeting a reality.

Go back and read about this meeting slowly and prayerfully. Take special note of all the maneuvering that took place in the spirit realm to bring the man of God into contact with this group of spiritually hungry people. First, God sends His angel in a vision while Cornelius is in prayer, telling him to send men to Joppa to find a man he never heard of and didn't know. He was told this man Peter *will tell you what you must do* (Acts 10:6). Cornelius obeys by sending three men on the two-day journey to find this person. The next day, as they're approaching the outskirts of the city, Peter is praying on the housetop, not knowing any of this has taken place. He falls into a trance that at first seems confusing and difficult to understand. He doesn't realize what's happening, but by the time the trance ends, God has made sure he knows enough to trust and obey.

As he meditates on what he has just experienced, there's a knock at the door. The three men sent by Cornelius have asked around, and have found Simon's house. They ask if a man named Peter is staying there. Meanwhile up on the housetop, as Peter is still pondering the meaning of the vision, the Holy Spirit speaks and says this: *"Behold, three men are seeking you. Arise therefore, go down and go with them, doubting nothing; for I have sent them"* (Acts 10:19-20). They proceed to tell Peter that Cornelius their master saw an angel, and was told to come get him so that *when he comes, he will speak to you* (Acts 10:32). In obedience to the Holy Spirit's instructions, Peter takes six other Jewish Christians and sets off for Cornelius' house.

I love what it says next: *And the following day they entered Caesarea. Now Cornelius **was waiting for them**, and had called together his relatives and close friends* (Acts 10:24). Peter comes in and finds many people gathered together, waiting for him. *Waiting for what? Words!* It is at this point that Peter understands the meaning of the trance he experienced on Simon's housetop in Joppa. These people are Gentiles, not Jews. Up until then, the Jews believed that in order to be saved, you had to become a Jew. Even the Jewish Christians believed that, until what happened, happened that day.

ENTRUSTED WITH A STEWARDSHIP

This is why God did the supernatural things He did to arrange this meeting, giving His entrusted bondservant the opportunity to share the words of eternal life with these precious people. From then on, the saints understood that God's plan of salvation had *always* included Jew and Gentile alike. An angel appeared to Cornelius and told him he needed to hear words from Peter (Acts 10:22). Meanwhile, during his regular time of prayer, Peter fell into a trance that he didn't immediately understand, and simultaneously, Gentile messengers are sent from a far-away city to find a born again Jew who, as far as God is concerned, understands what it means to be entrusted with a stewardship. Because Peter does what he's told to do, the results are spiritually astounding. Not only does an entire household of people get saved, but the gospel itself is launched into the entire Gentile world, impacting and saving millions and millions of people from then until now.

Let me emphasize once again the fact that when the angel first appeared to Cornelius, he was told he needed to hear *from a man*. Think about that! An angel of God is standing in front of this unsaved man, but can't tell him how he and his household are to be saved! A man was needed to do that. A man of God entrusted not just with the gospel, but with the spiritual understanding to be the steward God needed him to be.

WE NEED TO UNDERSTAND

Teach me, O Lord, the way of Your statues, and I shall keep it to the end. **Give me understanding**, *and I shall keep Your law; indeed, I shall observe it with my whole heart.*

—Psalms 119:34

In the epistles, the Holy Spirit gives us inspired prayers to pray. They can be found mainly in the books of Ephesians, Philippians, and

Colossians. The importance of developing spiritual understanding is included as an important item to pray for in each prayer. Here are a few examples:

> *Therefore I also, after I heard of your faith in the Lord Jesus and your love for all the saints, do not cease to give thanks for you, making mention of you in my prayers: that the God of our Lord Jesus Christ, the father of glory, may give to you the spirit of wisdom and revelation in the knowledge of Him,* **the eyes of your understanding being enlightened.** . . .
>
> —Ephesians 1:15-18

> *Praying always with all prayer and supplication in the Spirit,* **being watchful to this end** *with all perseverance and supplication for all the saints.*
>
> —Ephesians 6:18

> *For this reason we also, since the day we heard it, do not cease to pray for you, and to ask that you may be filled with the knowledge of His will in all wisdom and* **spiritual understanding**.
>
> —Colossians 1:9

SET HIGH STANDARDS

When believers start walking with daily awareness of these things, they will self-regulate. They value the importance of having others alongside to encourage or correct, if necessary, but they do most of the personal spiritual monitoring themselves. They will purpose with all their heart to be players, not just spectators. They will be participants, not just sideline critics. As children of God entrusted with the gospel, they will understand the importance of setting high standards of excellence they hold themselves to.

> Not that I have already attained, or am already perfected; but I press on, that I may lay hold of that for which Christ Jesus has also laid hold of me. Brethren, I do not count myself to have apprehended; but one thing I do, **forgetting** those things which are behind and **reaching forward** to those things which are ahead, I **press** toward the goal for the prize of **the upward call of God** in Christ Jesus. Therefore let us, as many as are mature, have this mind; and if in anything you think otherwise, God will reveal even this to you.
>
> —Philippians 3:12-15

It's not what we say or do in public that determines our useability before God. It's what we say or do privately—that's what matters to God. All through the scriptures, the Bible talks about secrets and secret things. Secret things of God (Deuteronomy 29:29), and the secrets of men (Romans 2:16). Christians who understand that being entrusted with the gospel means we are also entrusted with the stewardship of monitoring every aspect of their daily lives. No secret sins allowed or tolerated. We must make sure we are right where we need to be, running our race in the specific lane God has chosen for us. We can't allow any spiritual drifting from the standards described in the Bible—the standards of excellence we set for ourselves.

Ours is the *upward call*, and it is precious in the sight of God. It's never to be taken lightly, or taken for granted. It's the prize we get on the day of our judgment, when we hear Jesus say to us: *"Well done, good and faithful servant"* (Matthew 25:21,23), and when we hear God say to us what He said about Jesus: *"This is my beloved son, in whom I am well pleased"* (Matthew 17:5; Luke 3:22).

ONE WAY OR THE OTHER—DO IT

> *For if I do this willingly, I have a reward; but if against my will, I have been **entrusted with a stewardship**.*
>
> —1 Corinthians 9:17

What have believers been entrusted with from God? *Stewardship.* Here's the dictionary.com definition for that word: *Stewardship as a noun*:

1. The position and duties of a <u>steward</u>, a person who acts as the surrogate of another or others, especially by managing property, financial affairs, an estate, etc.

2. The responsible overseeing and protection of something considered worth caring for and preserving.

    Synonyms for the word "stewardship:" control, protection, supervision, trust, administration, charge, keeping, safekeeping, custody, management, care, executing, guiding, governing, admonishing, organizing, and overseeing.

All of these definitions and synonyms are good and accurate, but I especially like definition #2: *The responsible overseeing and protection of something considered worth caring for and preserving.* Do you think the Word of God, the gospel, the lifesaving, life-changing message of salvation, the only hope given from God to avoid His eternal wrath and punishment for our sins in hell—is something worth caring for, promoting, and preserving? I think so! Not only that, but I think the gospel of the Lord Jesus is not just worth our care, promotion and preservation—it's also worth us living sanctified, God-fearing lives. Never forget what the Bible says is our responsibility in life. We are God's chosen vessels to preach, teach, and give warning to every human being. This must be done from a position of holiness, purity, and total dedication to the cause—as commanded by the Lord Himself (Mark 16:15-18).

> *Paul, a bondservant of Jesus Christ, called to be an apostle, **separated** to the gospel of God.*
>
> —Romans 1:1

> *Come, my people, enter your chambers, and **shut your doors behind you. Hide yourself**, as it were, for a little moment, until the indignation is past.*
>
> —Isaiah 26:20

If we walk with spiritual understanding in this life, we will understand that we're entrusted with a stewardship. It is imperative our priorities are established upon this truth.

CHAPTER 7

ENTRUSTED WITH GOD'S PEOPLE

Shepherd the flock of God *which is among you, serving as overseers, not by compulsion but willingly, not for dishonest gain but eagerly; nor as being lords* **over those entrusted to you**, *but being examples to the flock.*

—1 Peter 5:2-3

Sanctify them *by Your truth. Your word is truth. As You sent Me into the world, I also have sent them into the world. And* **for their sakes** *I sanctify Myself, that* **they also** *may be sanctified by the truth.*

—John 17:17-19

We can't lead others by example until we consistently lead ourselves. First John 3:18 says it best: *"My little children, let us not love in word or in tongue, but in deed and in truth."* In other words, put up or shut up. Don't try to talk the talk until you walk the walk. The best way to prioritize this is to major on what I call "the big three."

Entrusted for Eternity

*And now abide **faith, hope, love**, these three, but the greatest of these is love.*

—1 Corinthians 13:13

Because we're entrusted with the gospel, we *owe* it to the world to develop daily proficiency in these three areas, especially in the area of divine love. Many great books have been written on these subjects, and I've done so myself in my writings, so we won't go into detail here. What we will detail here is the need to understand *why* these three subjects are so important. We're entrusted, so we need to walk by faith and not by sight (2 Corinthians 5:7). We're entrusted, so we need to protect our hope, and share our hope with others (Psalms 42:5,11). We're entrusted, so we need to walk in love, as Jesus commanded (John 13:34-35).

Being entrusted with the gospel means we are no longer living a selfish life centered upon us and our desires. According to 2 Timothy 2:3-5, we became soldiers in the army of the Lord when we got saved. That means we were also instructed to sanctify ourselves for the Lord's sake—and for the sake of those He sends us to. The intercessory prayer Jesus prayed In John Chapter 17 tells us exactly what He was here to do, and what we're now supposed to be doing as His ambassadors (2 Corinthians 5:21). An ambassador is an official representative of the country who sends them. That's us today, as members of the Body of Christ. We take the time to separate from the world's lusts and distractions, and focus entirely on the mission at hand—worldwide evangelism.

This is why we're told to study to show ourselves *approved* (2 Timothy 2:15 KJV), workers who won't be ashamed when standing before God on our judgment day (Romans 14:10; 2 Corinthians 5:10). Approved to do what, exactly? To study God's Word and fill our hearts with the spiritual understanding necessary to resist the selfish impulses and desires of our dead-to-sin flesh. This enables us to concentrate on the task we've been entrusted to fulfill, and carry on with the mission Jesus came to initiate. He left heaven, came to Earth in the form of a human bondservant, lived a sin-free life and went to the cross as God's spotless Lamb—taking away the sin and sins of the world (John 1:29; Revelation 1:5). Now, as entrusted Christians, we must discipline ourselves to see and reveal the unseen world so that unsaved people will have their spiritual eyes opened to the truth.

> *That Christ may dwell in your hearts through faith; that you, **being rooted and grounded in love,** may be able to comprehend with all the saints what is the **width and length and depth and height**. . . .*
>
> —Ephesians 3:17-18

Notice our comprehension of these four things must be done in partnership with all the other saints. In other words, we need each other. We need a unified effort to present the truth to the world. *Everybody needs everybody else.* Nobody in the Body of Christ is an island unto themselves. We all need to grow and work together to understand the scope of these four words—width, length, depth, and height. They refer to the "big picture" of eternity.

WIDTH DEALS WITH STUDY BALANCE

We must be "well-rounded" on all important Bible topics. Christians have various challenges and needs, and we're not a bunch of clones or robots. That's why we need a broad understanding on all the major topics found in the Bible. That's not to say we must become noted scholars on these subjects, but we all should have a working understanding of what they are and how they relate to one another. I've met people who spend all their time on one or two subjects from the Bible. They may know some things as long as they stay within their limited scope of biblical understanding, but get them out beyond their pet topics and they're useless as far as God is concerned.

As I've already stated: we need a working knowledge of the "big three" of faith, hope, and love (1 Corinthians 13:13). That's a great place to start, but there's much more to discover! In Hebrews 6:1-2, Paul talks about the six foundational topics every baby Christian should know. 1) Repentance from dead works. 2) Faith towards God. 3) The doctrine of baptisms. 4) Laying on of hands. 5) Resurrection of the dead. 6) Eternal judgment. In Ephesians 6:10-20, the Bible reveals the scope of spiritual warfare, who our enemies are, and how we defeat them with the weapons God has made available to us. It is very important we know these things, and share them with those whom God has entrusted us with.

LENGTH DEALS WITH TIME AWARENESS

We must know where we are on God's dispensational calendar. All the dispensations are important, but the Bible tells us to be established in the *present* truth (2 Peter 1:12). The present truth is the dispensation of grace, otherwise called the church age. That is the age we are living in now. The Bible says to look up, because our redemption draws near. That means this dispensation is rapidly coming to a close. Therefore, our attitude must be one of excited anticipation, not doom, gloom, fear, and dread.

Yes, Jesus could return today. All prophetic signs pointing to the rapture of the Church have been fulfilled. World events and what's happening across the social and political spectrum indicate the same. However, understanding the rapture could happen at any moment isn't an excuse to sit around wasting time—as some rapture critics think. To the contrary, the Bible says we are to comfort one another with these words (1 Thessalonians 4:18). How often? More and more with each passing day (Hebrews 10:25). That means we're supposed to be walking out our salvation everyday with excitement and a true sense of purpose (1 Thessalonians 4:1-12).

Think about this. If Jesus Christ appeared to you *today*, and told you He was coming back for the Church one week from now, would you just sit around eating chips and salsa, praising the Lord? Of course not! You'd be like every other born again believer who loves God and wants to see others saved. You'd be on the phone calling or texting everyone you know—imploring them to make things right with God before it's too late. Well, that's exactly why these verses are found in the Word of God! Every Christian should live each day with the awareness that time is short. Don't be like those Peter describes in his letter to his congregants:

> Knowing this first; that **scoffers will come in the last days**, walking according to their own lusts, and saying, "Where is the promise of His coming? For since the fathers fell asleep, all things continue as they were from the beginning of creation."
>
> —2 Peter 3:3-4

Read all of 2 Peter 3, and you'll get the picture. Be ready. Stay ready. And tell others to do the same.

DEPTH REFERS TO OUR ATTITUDE TOWARD OTHERS

Being entrusted with God's people means we see them as precious in the eyes of the Lord, and we do whatever we can to help them stay focused on the big picture of eternity. We know we're all equally loved by God, so we avoid the temptations to lift ourselves up in pride. As it also says in Luke 10:27, we love our neighbor as ourselves. We don't judge or condemn them. We're gentle and patient, like loving parents would be with their own children (1 Thessalonians 2:7).

HEIGHT REFERS TO OUR ATTITUDE TOWARD GOD

Our attitude toward God must be one of obedience based on our love for Him. We love Him and pledge our lives to Him in loyal service. Because we're entrusted with God's people, they need to see and hear us living lives that demonstrate our commitment to the Lord and the Great Commission of Mark 16:15-18 and Matthew 28:18-20. This is what it means to love the Lord our God with all our heart, soul, strength, and mind (Luke 10:27). This also means we maintain the right attitude when we come boldly to God's throne of grace (Hebrews 4:16). We don't just barge into the throne room and start spouting off in anger, impatience, and frustration. We approach our heavenly Father with great respect, no matter what's going on in our lives at the moment. The Book of Ecclesiastes says it best:

> *Do not be **rash** with your mouth, and let not your heart utter anything **hastily** before God. For God is in heaven, and you on earth; therefore **let your words be few**.*
>
> —Ecclesiastes 5:2

We're entrusted to keep the big picture in front of the brethren we are surrounded with. We should be exhorting one another, not discouraging one another (Hebrews 10:25). The Bible says to look up, because our redemption draws near (Luke 21:25-28). As we keep our eyes on the horizon, we should be encouraging others to do the same. That end-times attitude must be paramount in how we relate to one another in the Body of Christ.

FEED HIS LAMBS AND SHEEP

> *So when they had eaten breakfast, Jesus said to Simon Peter, "Simon, son of Jonah, do you love Me more than these?" He*

said to Him, "Yes, Lord; You know that I love you." He said to him, **"Feed My lambs."** *He said to him again a second time, "Simon, son of Jonah, do you love Me?" He said to Him, "Yes, Lord: You know that I love you." He said to him,* **"Tend My sheep."** *He said to him the third time, "Simon, son of Jonah, do you love Me?" Peter was grieved because He said to him the third time, "Do you love Me?" And he said to Him, "Lord, You know all things; You know that I love You." Jesus said to him,* **"Feed My sheep. . . ."**

—John 21:15-18

Those entrusted with God's people must accept the responsibility to feed fellow Christians with the milk and meat of God's Word (Hebrews 5:12-14). Peter was being told to do both. Once again, this doesn't just apply to those called into the full-time ministries of apostle, prophet, evangelist, pastor, or teacher (Ephesians 4:11). We are all called to be God's ambassadors, spreading the Word of God as led by the Holy Spirit. That being said, it behooves us to take our responsibilities seriously, not casually as is the manner of many. *Sheep need to be fed to be led.* That applies to the babes in Christ (the lambs), and the older saints (the sheep). This is not just the job of those called into leadership positions. Its every believer's job and responsibility, to one degree or another. Discipleship is needed at every level inside the Body of Christ. We must never allow ourselves to become lifted up in pride, thinking we know all there is to know about serving God. That is a recipe for disaster. Stay teachable, and be armed and ready to teach, exhort, and assist with all patience (2 Timothy 4:2-5).

CHAPTER 8

ENTRUSTED TO BE LEAN, MEAN, AND CLEAN

God has given us His Word to show us the way to salvation, and the lifestyle we live afterward. The three words used for the title of this chapter were given to me years ago from the Lord. Being entrusted with the gospel is an honor that carries with it the responsibility to be examples to the sheep of God's pasture. We need to be lean, mean, and clean for three entities. First, we need to live this way for God. Second, we need to live this way for others—both saints and sinner alike. Third, we need to live this way for ourselves. There is no way we can effectively represent Jesus as a heavenly ambassador (2 Corinthian 5:20) without these three words being the anchor of our souls. Paul addressed this when he wrote his letter to the Roman believers, many of which were Jews.

> *Indeed you are called a Jew, and rest on the law, and make your boast in God, and know His will, and approve the things*

that are excellent, being instructed out of the law, and are confident that you yourself are a guide to the blind, a light to those who are in darkness, and instructor of the foolish, a teacher of babes, having the form of knowledge and truth in the law. You, therefore, who teach another, **do you not teach yourself?** *You who preach that a man should not steal,* **do you** *steal? You who say, "Do not commit adultery,"* **do you** *commit adultery? You who abhor idols,* **do you** *rob temples? You who make your boast in the law,* **do you** *dishonor God through breaking the law?*

—Romans 2:17-23

This is just one excerpt from Paul's letter to the Roman Christians. Carefully read all of Romans Chapter 2, and you'll see he doesn't just rail on the hypocrisy of the Jewish saints. He admonishes the Gentile Christians in the same way. Jew or Gentile, he is telling all of them to practice what they preach, and to shut up and sit down until they do. Why is there so much about this in the Word of God? Because we've been entrusted with all of this, that's why.

Paul was lean. He didn't allow the lust of the flesh, the lust of the eyes, and the pride of life to pollute his personal walk with God (1 John 2:16). *Paul was mean.* He was passionate about defending the truth, not just to the unsaved religious puppets of the devil, but also to some of the most anointed and influential leaders in the Body of Christ (Acts 23:2-3; Galatians 2:11-16). *Paul was clean.* He kept his body under control, even though like with all of us, there were times when his flesh wanted to rebel (1 Corinthians 9:27; Romans Chapters 6 and 7). Like Paul, we're entrusted to be lean, mean, and clean for Jesus. There is no other way to proclaim the whole counsel of God, especially in today's world of mediocrity, carnality, and compromise—not just in the world, but inside the Body of Christ as well.

ENTRUSTED TO BE LEAN, MEAN, AND CLEAN

Jesus did something none of us could ever do. Even though the assignment God entrusted Him with was carried out without any missteps or sin, the four gospels are in the Bible to provide us with the perfect template to use as the goal to shoot for. Jesus set the bar high, but bondservants like Paul proved we can get close enough to that bar to make a significant impact in our world of influence. Being lean, mean, and clean can make the difference in the lives of multitudes of people. What joy it is to know we're entrusted to be directly involved in helping Jesus turn people from darkness to light, and from the power of Satan to the power of God (Acts 26:16-18). There can be no greater honor than this!

Never forget this truth: the further you want to go with God, the fewer your options become!

THE WIDE ROAD AND NARROW GATE

> "Enter by the **narrow** gate; for **wide** is the gate and **broad** is the way that leads to destruction, and there are **many** who go in by it. Because **narrow** is the gate and **difficult** is the way which leads to life, and there are **few** who find it."
>
> —Matthew 7:13-14

The gate that leads to heaven and eternal life is a narrow one, because God has a righteous standard that transcends all generations, cultures, and nationalities. And in this age of rampant sin, Christian compromise, and mass-mediocrity, we would be wise to remember that fact. Salvation starts and ends with Jesus (John 14:6). Period. And from that point, our walk with God will progressively take us down an ever-narrowing road that's difficult to navigate. Narrow means limited choices in this life. Difficult means its challenging when living in a body that doesn't want to serve God (Romans 7:15-25). If we understand that we've been entrusted with the gospel, we understand what it will take to be strong and stay strong for Jesus.

God will always love us, and will always be there to help us navigate the difficult road and enter eternal life through His narrow gate. But He can only work with our choices that line up with His Word (Psalms 37:4-5). Entrusted Christians must make the decision to live by His rules, and no one else's. When we decide to take our relationship with Him to a higher level of sanctification, purpose, focus and purity, the blessings and favor of God will increase proportionately. That takes character and commitment because we're in the world but not of the world (John 17:16). Jesus said the road to death and destruction is wide and easy, and most people go that way—*because its wide and easy!* And even inside the Body of Christ, too many believers are always looking for the easy-to-navigate, well-paved road in life. Very seldom do they look to travel on the right road, because its narrow, full of potholes, and harder to navigate. The *only* way to God's blessings in this life, and eternal life afterwards is Jesus. Don't ever let the devil or anyone else tell you otherwise.

I'm reminded of one of my Old Testament heroes of faith—Caleb. When I get to heaven, I'm going to look for this guy! When it came time to divvy up the promised land, Caleb told Joshua he wanted the mountain as his property inheritance. Why? Because the giants were still up there, and he had been itching to fight them for the past 45 years (Joshua 14:10-12). He didn't want the beach front property. He didn't want the villa along the golf course. He didn't want the plush city condo. He didn't want the big ranch out west. He wanted the mountain! Why? Because he wanted to attack and drive out the giants, who by the way, were so large the 10 unbelieving spies had likened themselves to grasshoppers in comparison (Numbers 13:31-33). And here's another tidbit to chew on—the man was 85 years old when he put in his request! Is it any wonder God called this man a man with a *different spirit* in him, a man who *followed God fully* (Numbers 14:24)? This man knew what kind of attitude and lifestyle it took to navigate the narrow road. We need to live like he did—traveling the narrow road as lean, mean, clean fighting machines for Jesus. Entrusted believers know this, and refuse to entertain any teachings or doctrines that say otherwise.

JESUS SET THE BAR

> Let nothing be done through selfish ambition or conceit, but in lowliness of mind let each esteem others better than himself. Let each of you look out not only for his own interests, but also for the interests of others. Let this mind be in you **which was also in Christ Jesus**, who being in the form of God, did not consider it robbery to be equal with God, but **made himself** of no reputation, taking the form of a **bondservant** and coming in the likeness of men.
>
> —Philippians 2:3-7

> Therefore, when He came into the world, He said: "Sacrifice and offering you did not desire, but a body You have prepared for Me. In burnt offerings and sacrifices for sin You had no pleasure. Then I said, 'Behold, I have come—in the volume of the book it is written of Me—**to do Your will**, O God.'"
>
> —Hebrews 10:5-7

> But He said to them, "Let us go into the next towns, that I may preach there also, because **for this purpose** I have come forth.
>
> —Mark 1:38

*But He said to them, "I must preach the kingdom of God to the other cities also, because **for this purpose** I have been sent."*

—Luke 4:43

*"Now My soul is troubled, and what shall I say? 'Father, save Me from this hour'? But **for this purpose** I came to this hour."*

—John 12:27

*He who sins is of the devil, for the devil has sinned from the beginning. **For this purpose** the Son of God was manifested, that He might destroy the works of the devil.*

—1 John 3:8

From birth until death, Jesus knew He was entrusted with a purpose—to save us from our sins and destroy the works of the devil. He knew how much God loved us—wanting all men to be saved and come to the knowledge of the truth (John 3:16; 2 Peter 3:9). He knew He had come to earth to fulfill His Father's will and pave the way for our redemption. He knew that was His purpose, and wanted nothing else but to fulfill that purpose. He knew why He came and what He wanted out of life—and the discipline necessary to stay on God's narrow road to obtain it.

Our Lord's level of discipline is the gold standard for all of us. That's what made Him as strong as He was. Jesus was tempted in all points like we are, but He never sinned (Hebrews 4:15). In addition, He faced stronger temptations that we'll never have to face. Only Jesus could save us, but doing what had to be done to meet the demands for divine justice wasn't easy. Paying for our sins was an *extremely difficult road* that led to an *extremely narrow gate*. Read and meditate on our Lord's Garden of Gethsemane passion. We've never experienced pressure to disobey God like Jesus did in that garden. His level of stress and agony was so intense His sweat became like great drops of blood (Luke 22:44). If you understand the level of pain and suffering a victim endures when being crucified to death, you understand the magnitude of that temptation! Not only that, but He faced the prospect of being forsaken by God when our sins were laid on Him. That meant spending 3 days and nights in hell (Matthew 27:46; 2 Corinthians 5:21; Acts 2:27-31; Hebrews 1:3) to purge our sins and set us free. Our Lord could've called upon twelve legions of angels to deliver Him from the crucifixion experience, but He didn't (Matthew 26:53). He knew what He wanted, and through all the pain and suffering, remembered His life's purpose (Hebrews 2:14-15, 10:4-10)! We need to live our life like He lived His. There's no other way.

CHAPTER 9

ENTRUSTED WITH THE WORK OF DISCIPLINE

*So Jesus said to them again, "Peace to you! As the Father has sent Me, **I also send you.**"*

—John 20:21

*Most assuredly, I say to you, he who believes in Me, the works that I do, he will do also; and **greater works** than these he will do, because I go to My Father.*

—John 14:12

When it comes to spiritual reality, life is simple. It can be summed up in three points. First, Jesus was entrusted with the task of saving the human race, and succeeded. Second, we're now entrusted with telling this wonderful truth to the world, and continue to do so. Third, the devil will do whatever it takes to stop us, as long as he is on the earth. That sums up *everything*.

As believers committed to the cause, we understand we're entrusted with the responsibility to lead others as we lead ourselves. This is what Paul was addressing when he chastised the believers in the Roman Church. We can't lead others along the difficult road and through the narrow salvation gate unless we ourselves are disciplined to set the example and inspire others to do the same.

With that fact in mind, I've come to understand that when Jesus sent us and told us to do the "works" that He did, it's not just the work of miracles, signs and wonders. It also includes the work of daily, personal discipline. After all, if we're not disciplined with our spiritual *and* physical affairs, we'll never be in position to see Jesus perform the works that confirm the message we share (Mark 16:19-20). Paul talked about this often in his letters to the churches.

> *Truly the signs of an apostle were accomplished among you **with all perseverance** in signs and wonders and mighty deeds.*
>
> —2 Corinthians 12:12

> *But I **discipline my body** and **bring it into subjection**, lest, when I have preached to others, I myself should become disqualified.*
>
> —1 Corinthians 9:27

> *I affirm, by the boasting in you which I have in Christ Jesus our Lord, **I die daily**.*
>
> —1 Corinthians 15:31

Even though Paul was mightily used by God in supernatural ways throughout his ministry, he still had the responsibility to maintain control over his own flesh. His struggles in this area are well documented

ENTRUSTED WITH THE WORK OF DISCIPLINE

in Romans Chapters 6 and 7. Because he knew he had been entrusted with the gospel, he knew how important it was to stay on that narrow and difficult road consistently. It's a daily discipline we must all embrace, and it's not easy. If it were easy, every Christian would be doing it, but they're not. Yes, Jesus said His yoke was easy and His burden was light (Matthew 11:28-30), but the only way we find that kind of rest for our souls is *after* we develop and maintain discipline over our flesh. As Paul put it—we consistently die daily. That is, we bring the body's lusts and desires under control, and keep them suppressed day in and day out. If we don't, we'll experience the same kind of frustrations many Christians experience consistently. They love God but their flesh keeps getting in the way!

God's commands are *commands*, not requests or suggestions. It doesn't matter what men say about this. It only matters what God says. He decided to entrust us with His word, and the assignments for outreach that go with it. He said we should be holy because He is (1 Peter 1:13-19). He also told us to sanctify ourselves in spirit, soul, and body (1 Thessalonians 5:23), especially in the area of sex (1 Thessalonians 4:3). That demands discipline, and that's how we travel the *only road* that leads to the *only gate* leading to eternal life.

DIFFICULT DOES NOT MEAN IMPOSSIBLE

When the Bible says the salvation gate is narrow and journey to reach it is difficult, it doesn't mean it's impossible to navigate and acquire. It simply means its challenging to stay lean, mean, and clean when we are surrounded by sin, filth, compromise, mediocrity, and servants of Satan everywhere. But separated we must stay—because we've been entrusted with the gospel. The Lord also said that only a few will measure up to this standard of performance. Not many professing

Christians will be qualified to be used by God in these last days, but I intend to be included in that list. I hope that's a priority for you, too.

God has a righteous standard for all believers that transcends all generations, cultures, and nationalities. And in this dark and evil world, we would be wise to remember that fact. People say that there are many ways to God. They also say we are all children of God. Statements like those do nothing but demonstrate a level of spiritual ignorance on display for all the world to see. The Word of God says something completely different. If a person wants to make heaven their home some day when they die, the gate they pass through is narrow and road they travel to get there is even narrower. That simply means there are *not* many ways to God. We quote John 14:6 once again: "Jesus is *the* way, *the* truth, and *the* life." No one comes to God any other way, or through anyone else. It also means those who are entrusted with the gospel must live their lives with razor-sharp focus and clarity. Like Jesus, we should be able to say what He said in John 14:30: *"The ruler of this world comes, but has nothing in me."* Our Lord described the salvation road as one with deep ditches on either side. Hypocrisy is one such ditch.

> *And He spoke a parable to them, "Can the blind lead the blind? Will they not both fall into the ditch? A disciple is not above his teacher, but everyone who is perfectly trained will be like this teacher. And why do you look at the speck in your brother's eye, but do not perceive* **the plank in your own eye**? *Or how can you say to your brother, 'Brother, let me remove the speck that is in your eye,' when you yourself do not* **see the plank that is in your own eye? Hypocrite!** *First* **remove the plank** *from your own eye, and then you will see clearly to remove the speck that is in your brother's eye."*
>
> —Luke 6:39-42

ENTRUSTED WITH THE WORK OF DISCIPLINE

Salvation starts and ends with Jesus, and we've been charged by God to tell that truth to the world. With such awesome responsibility, we must understand that the Holy Spirit is going to lead us through a very narrow gate, and down an ever-narrowing road that culminates in our homegoing to heaven! This realization is a pre-requisite for being the lean, mean, and clean soldier of Christ entrusted with the gospel (2 Timothy 2:1-7). When we decide to take our relationship with Him to a higher level of sanctified purpose, the blessings and favor of God increase proportionately. The wide gate and easy road leads to death and destruction. It is the wrong way. The narrow gate and challenging road leads to salvation and eternal life. It is the right way. We are entrusted with this truth, and told to share it everywhere. No apologies. No regrets. No options.

> *For I have not shunned to declare to you the **whole counsel of God**.*
>
> —Acts 20:27

> *From Miletus he sent to Ephesus and called for the elders of the church. And when they had come to him, he said to them: "You know, from the first day that I came to Asia, in what manner I always lived among you, serving the Lord with all humility with many tears and trials which happened to me by the plotting of the Jews; **how I kept back nothing that was helpful**, but proclaimed it to you, and **taught you publicly and from house to house**, testifying to Jews, and also to Greeks, repentance toward God and faith toward our Lord Jesus Christ."*
>
> —Acts 20:18-21

The whole counsel of God means we preach, teach, and train people without apology, declaring every good and perfect gift that comes down from the Father of lights (James 1:17). We do not shy away from the blunt truth of heaven, hell, life, death, and the clear standards that God shows us concerning the way, the truth, and the life that only Jesus can provide. There is a long list of martyrs who have given their lives for this very reason, and who still do so today in many places. Because we're entrusted with the gospel, we dare not give in to the temptation to alter our message under pressure or threat in anyway. Look around and see what's happening worldwide. Persecution against believers is increasing everywhere, and it might show up on your doorstep sooner than later. If and when it does, are you prepared to stand your ground for Jesus without compromise, under threat of imprisonment, torture, and even death? Am I? These are questions every Christian must ask and answer before the Lord.

Paul was very adamant about this, even going so far as to declare a curse upon anyone who tried to use false doctrine to pollute the minds of the Galatian brethren (Galatians 1:9). We must never lower the bar and compromise the truth. The responsibility is too great. Paul never allowed the sufferings he endured to dissuade him from giving believers everything they needed to know to live a triumphant life. Read about all he suffered in 2 Corinthians Chapters 1, 4, 6, and 11. When Jesus told Ananias that Paul would suffer greatly for preaching in the name of Jesus, He wasn't kidding (Acts 9:15). Even so, Paul refused to back off from teaching the whole counsel of God. As a result, he could declare his victory to Timothy, and to all of us today. He fought the good fight, ran his race to completion and kept the faith without wavering (2 Timothy 4:7). I want to be able to say the same thing. How about you?

REMEMBER WHAT YOU WANT MOST

God's road is uphill and challenging, and His gate is narrow. From start to finish, make sure you're strong enough to stay on the Lord's

ENTRUSTED WITH THE WORK OF DISCIPLINE

Road, and slim enough to fit through His gate! There's no other way we can live victoriously, or lead others to victory. All of this can be summed up in one word: *discipline*. There are many definitions for discipline that you could study and apply, but the core element for maintaining a disciplined life is simple. *Discipline is remembering what you want most!* There is a heaven to gain and a hell to shun, and we get to choose which place becomes our eternal home. Not only that, but we get to choose *how* we travel the winding road, and pass through His narrow gate. We know we've been entrusted with the gospel. We know we've been commanded to take it into all the world. We also know we'll stand before the Lord someday to have our lives judged by His word. So, here's what all of us should want to hear as the reward for a life that's been lean, mean, and clean for Jesus. *"Well done, good and faithful servant; you were faithful over a few things, I will make you ruler over many things. Enter into joy of your lord"* (Matthew 25:21,25). Picture that moment in your mind, and keep those words from the Lord as the end-game goal of your life—especially when you're faced with compromise in any area of your daily walk with God.

Never forget this truth: A true disciple of Christ will always give up what he wants today, for what he wants most tomorrow.

CHAPTER 10

ENTRUSTED TO REPLICATE

Therefore I urge you, **imitate me**.

—1 Corinthians 4:16

Imitate me*, just as I also imitate Christ.*

—1 Corinthians 11:1

The things which you learned and received and heard and saw in me, ***these do****, and the God of peace will be with you.*

—Philippians 4:9

Paul told his disciples to imitate him as he imitated Christ. Can any of us say the same thing to those who know us as Christians today? I'm sorry to say that one of the greatest hindrances to world evangelism are the shallow lifestyles, carnal activities, and selfish priorities of people claiming to be Christian. When I was unsaved and in the world of corporate advertising, I thought there couldn't be an environment any more cut-throat. *Then I was called into full-time ministry!* Wow!

What an eye-opener it was for me! I found out that the carnal, sinful level of life within the ranks of the corporate community was "Candy Land" compared to all the junk Christians immerse themselves in every day. That's a good question we need to be asking ourselves, as we stand before the mirror in our prayer closets. Do we inspire anyone to raise the bar in their lives, and serve Jesus like we do? We've been entrusted with the gospel, so we should be an inspiration to those who see us and know us.

SHOW OTHERS THE WAY

Notice the four areas of example Paul set for his sons and daughters in faith. If we're walking in the light of our responsibilities to protect and present the gospel like he did, these four elements must be in play. *First, they learned.* That means he taught them accurately from the Word of God. *Second, they received.* That means he imparted to them spiritual gifts and blessings from the Lord. *Third, they heard.* That means Paul's reputation was widespread. They knew his ministry was effectively challenging the people wherever he went for Jesus. Many loved him and many hated him, but everyone knew him and what he stood for. *Fourth, they saw.* They watched him live the life, not just talk the talk. In other words, do what's right whether you feel like it or not. One way or the other—just do it!

LIVING THE BALANCED LIFE

*But beware lest somehow this liberty of yours **become a stumbling block** to those who are weak.*

—1 Corinthians 8:9

*Stand fast therefore in the **liberty** by which Christ has made us free, and do not be entangled again with a yoke of bondage. For you brethren, have been **called to liberty**, only **do not** use liberty as an **opportunity for the flesh**, but through love serve one another.*

—Galatians 5:1,13

*"Conscience," I say, not your own, but **that of the other**. For why is my liberty judged by another man's conscience?*

—1 Corinthians 10:29

Brother Kenneth E. Hagin used to always talk about Christians who keep falling into ditches on either side of the road of life. His point was one of spiritual balance. Yes, we've been freed from the constraints of religious law, and thank God for that! That was the problem with the Pharisees in our Lord's time, and which is the problem with many Christian denominations today. On the other hand, we've been entrusted with the responsibility to be good stewards of the gospel—for the Lord first, for others second, and for ourselves third. That means we have to find the balance between spiritual freedom and carnal discipline.

STANDING FOR RIGHTEOUSNESS PRIVATLEY

One could devote an entire book on the subject, but that's not my assignment in writing this book. But in brief, we need to remember that as believers who lead other believers, God isn't the only One watching and listening. People are as well, even if they deny the fact. Paul's letters spoke extensively about these things, especially to carnal Christian churches like the Corinthian and Galatian churches. Each of us has to seek the Lord and find His balance in our lives regarding what we can or cannot do as Christians. There are certain things that are sinful to one Christian that to another they aren't, even though both are believers serving the Lord. Paul addresses this in his letter to the Romans:

> Receive one who is weak in the faith, but not to **disputes over doubtful things**. For one believes he may eat all things, but he who is weak eats only vegetables. Let not him who eats despise him who does not eat, and let not him who does not eat judge him who eats, for God has received him. Who are you to judge another's servant? To his own master he stands or falls. Indeed, he will be made to stand, for God is able to make him stand. One person esteems one day above another, another esteems every day alike. **Let every man be fully convinced in his own mind.** But why do you judge your brother? Or why do you show contempt for your brother? For we shall all stand before the judgment seat of Christ. Do you have faith? Have it to yourself before God. Happy is he who does not condemn himself in what he approves.
>
> —Romans 14:1-5,10,22

Read the whole chapter of Romans 14, and you'll see more of what I've highlighted here. Paul was exhorting us to major on the majors, and minor on the minors. And in doing so, to avoid spending time judging others when we should be spending time judging ourselves. Don't forget what Jesus said about all of this in Matthew 7:3-5: if you've got "planks" in your eye, don't be so quick to point out specks in your brother's eye—until you deal with your own "planks" first. Jesus demonstrated this mindset when He was confronted with the woman caught in the act of adultery (John 8:2-11).

BIBLICAL DIVERSITY IS GOD'S IDEA

What's the point? It's simply this: the Body of Christ is a worldwide body of believers with different cultures and customs. Because we're entrusted to replicate ourselves for the sake of the gospel, we need to remember that believers in one country may or may not have the same personal lifestyle convictions as believers from another country—or even from other parts of the same country. Nevertheless, we're all still born again Christians, and God loves us all. We should never try to make clones or robots as disciples. Differing cultures and customs don't bother God, so why should they bother us? I've spent over four decades living and working in another country that has a very different cultural mindset. I learned a long time ago not to waste time trying to make people be just like me. Instead, I just "go with the flow," and let the Holy Spirit orchestrate the unique blend of personalities and nationalities.

Different languages say the same thing with differing words, and God loves the variety. Different cultures express themselves in different ways, and I think God finds that refreshing. There are different clothing standards worldwide for what is deemed appropriate and proper for Christians, and God understands that. Even though many things are constant across the board concerning biblical standards of right and wrong, many things differ because we're an international body of believers. Therefore, don't be so quick to argue or create division over personal convictions that don't matter in the scope of eternity in heaven or hell.

Case in point: in our travels in the Philippines and even in the U.S., when attending churches as a guest speaker, my wife has been stared at with obvious disdain simply because she takes the time to look as nice as possible for the church service. In and out of church, we've had so-called Christians judge her with their eyes, and talk about her behind our backs, as if she was the devil himself. And I'm thinking to myself, yeah, what a great witness that is to the world! As if God is actually going to deny someone entrance into heaven and let them descend into hell fire forever, simply because they violated some superficial standard of wardrobe etiquette. Really? Is that the God our Bible portrays? Ask the woman caught in adultery in John's gospel, as one example of what I'm talking about. I'm sure she'd have a different answer to those who run around judging everyone else's lifestyle except their own.

As the Word of God teaches us—what might be offensive to one believer may not be offensive to another, so we should give people the same space God gives us! We're talking here about individual culture and international lifestyle, because if you have taken a trip any farther than your neighborhood McDonald's restaurant, you'll find that not every Christian sees everything the same as you and I. We're not talking about obvious attempts to live a sinful and rebellious life in direct opposition to the clear standards of holiness of purity in the Bible. That's different altogether. But there are certain things that are called "doubtful things". These are things that differ but don't affect one's spiritual relationship with God.

> *Nevertheless the solid foundation of God stands, having this seal. "The Lord **knows those who are His**," and, "Let everyone who names the name of Christ depart from iniquity."*
>
> —2 Timothy 2:19

The Bible says God knows those who are His, and those who are His *don't want* to continue living sinful, rebellious lives anymore. If that's not the case, I question the sincerity of their "born again" experience.

CHAPTER 11

ENTRUSTED WITH FREE WILL

I call heaven and earth as witnesses today against you, that I have set before you life and death, blessing and cursing; **therefore choose life**, *that both you and your descendants may live.*

—Deuteronomy 30:19

The greatest weapon God has given to us is the power of choice. It's what we refer to as *free will*. Throughout the Bible the Lord reminds us of this, and exhorts us to choose wisely. In Matthew 12:34-37, Jesus said it as plainly as it could be said. *By our words we're justified and by our words we're condemned.* God won't make us say what He wants us to say, and the devil can't force us to say what he wants us to say. We choose our words, and those words chart our life on earth, and determine our eternal abode. That's why we need to realize the Bible is a book of words about words. God has commissioned multitudes of authors to write about this very thing, and I encourage you to fill your library with such material. I wrote an entire book on this subject myself, called *The Language of Faith*. I highly recommend it to you.

Because the Lord has entrusted us with the power of choice, it's up to each one of us to monitor our words, actions and choices every day. James 1:19 tells us to be *"swift to hear, slow to speak, and slow to wrath."* Proverbs 10:19 tells us that *"in the multitude of words sin is not lacking, but he who refrains his lips is wise."* In fact, I encourage you to read the books of Proverbs and James, and underline or highlight every verse that talks about the mouth, words, or anything connected to verbal expression. Trust me, you'll be doing a lot of highlighting when you do!

> *And the Spirit and the bride say, "Come!" And let him who hears say, "Come!" And let him who thirsts come.* ***Whoever desires****, let him take the water of life freely.*
>
> —Revelation 22:17

The "water of life" is freely offered to anyone who wants it, but to partake of it, we must make the right choices with the free will God has entrusted us with. Contrary to what many Christians teach and believe, God doesn't predetermine who gets saved and who doesn't. It's called foreknowledge, and it is the foundation that predestination is built upon. Romans 8:29 says it this way: *"For whom **He foreknew**, He also **predestined** to be conformed to the image of His Son, that He might be the firstborn among many brethren."* That simply means God knows the future, and knows ahead of time who will or won't make the decision to receive Jesus as Lord and Savior. As it says in Deuteronomy 30:19, He exhorts us to make the right choices regarding life, death, blessing, and cursing, but in the end, its left up to us to use our free will and make the choices. Jesus told us the same thing when He and Nicodemus had their after-dark conversation, as recorded in John Chapter 3.

ENTRUSTED WITH FREE WILL

*And as Moses lifted up the serpent in the wilderness, even so must the Son of Man be lifted up, that **whoever believes in Him** should not perish but have eternal life. For God so loved the world that He gave His only begotten Son, that **whoever believes in Him** should not perish but have everlasting life. He who believes in Him is not condemned; but he who does not believe is condemned already, because he has not believed in the name of the only begotten Son of God.*

—John 3:14-16,18

Whoever believes! This applies to everyone, not just to a certain few "lucky ones" that God selects. It's very revealing when you speak with Christians who believe that God picks and chooses who gets saved and who doesn't, because I've never met anyone who believes that who also believes they're not in the predetermined camp that gets to go to heaven! Hogwash! You and I have been entrusted with free will—unlimited free will. God lays out the whole scope of eternal reality in the Word of God. He tells us over and over to choose wisely, because He does not desire that *anyone perish* and go to hell (2 Peter 3:9). First Timothy 2:4 says it even more plainly. *"For this is good and acceptable in the sight of God our Savior, **who desires all men to be saved** and to come to the knowledge of the truth."* God wants every single human being to live an abundant life on earth (John 10:10), and spend eternity with Him after physical death. There you have it.

THE BIGGEST WORD

The biggest word in the English Bible is the two-letter word *if*. However this word is spelled in other languages, it still means "if." We can see this when we examine the list of blessings promised to those who choose to enter into covenant with God through Christ.

Entrusted for Eternity

> *And **if you are Christ's** then you are Abraham's seed, and heirs according to the promise.*
>
> —Galatians 3:29

Notice the word "if" in that verse. If we belong to Christ Jesus, it's because we chose to receive salvation by faith in what Jesus did for us on the cross. That choice automatically makes us the seed of Abraham, and heirs according to the promise. If we're not born again, that is, if we've chosen to reject the free gift of salvation by faith, we're not the seed of Abraham, and we're not heirs of the promise. Period. Deuteronomy Chapter 28 will give us an extensive list of the blessings and promises that come to us as Abraham's seed.

> *Now it shall come to pass, **if** you diligently obey the voice of the Lord your God, to observe carefully all His commandments which I command you today, that the Lord your God will set you high above all nations of the earth. And all these blessings shall come upon you and overtake you, **because** you obey the voice of the Lord your God: Blessed shall you be in the city, and blessed shall you be in the country. Blessed shall be the fruit of your body, the produce of your ground and the increase of your herds, the increase of your cattle and the offspring of your flocks. Blessed shall be your basket and you're your kneading bowl. Blessed shall you be when you come in, and blessed shall you be when you go out. The Lord will cause your enemies who rise against you to be defeated before your face; they shall come out against you one way and flee before you seven ways. The Lord will command the blessing on you in your storehouses and in all to which you set your hand, and He will bless you in the land which the Lord your God is giving you. The Lord will establish you as a holy people to Himself, just as He has sworn to you, **if** you keep the*

commandments of the Lord your God and walk in His ways. Then all peoples of the earth shall see that you are called by the name of the Lord, and they shall be afraid of you. And the Lord will grant you plenty of goods, in the fruit of your body, in the increase of your livestock, and in the produce of your ground, in the land of which the Lord swore to your fathers to give you. The Lord will open to you His good treasure, the heavens, to give the rain to your land in its season, and to bless all the work of your hand. You shall lend to many nations, but you shall not borrow. And the Lord will make you the head and not the tail; you shall be above only, and not be beneath, **if** *you heed the commandments of the Lord your God, which I command you today, and are careful to observe them. So you shall not turn aside from any of the words which I command you this day, to the right or the left, to go after other gods to serve them.*

—Deuteronomy 28:1-14

Notice the word "if" in these verses. It appears three times. Notice the word "because." It appears once, and basically means the same thing as the word "if." In those fourteen verses, these two words appear four times. Why? Because God wants us to realize the choices are all up to us. We can enjoy these blessings, or we can cut Him off with free will choices that prohibit Him from performing these wonderful promises on our behalf. Deuteronomy Chapter 28 contains sixty-eight verses. We've just highlighted the first fourteen verses. Those are the ones everyone likes to quote and believe for. But the rest of the chapter deals with the consequences for not choosing wisely when it comes to serving God.

Notice verse 15: *"But it shall come to pass,* **if** *you do not obey the voice of the Lord your God, to observe carefully all His commandments* *and His statutes which I command you today, that all these curses will come upon you and overtake you."* The list of curses and difficulties that come upon the person who chooses to disregard God's commandments is much longer than the list of blessings of obedience. Smart people will sit up and take notice of that truth.

CHAPTER 12

ENTRUSTED WITH VERBAL POWER

*Death and life are in **the power of the tongue**, and those who love it will eat its fruit.*

—Proverbs 18:21

This statement says it all in one verse. Going right along with God entrusting us with free will, we now see the responsibility of monitoring our mouth, because what we say determines how we live now, and where we live in eternity. In addition to what we find in the books of Proverbs and James, here's another precious nugget which we've highlighted already, but which bears repetition here.

*Walk prudently when you go to the house of God; and draw near to hear rather than to give the sacrifice of fools, for they do not know that they do evil. **Do not be rash with your mouth**, and let not your heart utter anything hastily before God. For God is in heaven and you on earth; **therefore let*** *your words be few. For a dream comes through much activity, and a fool's voice is known by his many words.*

—Ecclesiastes 5:1-3

When you study the Bible on this subject of being entrusted with verbal power, understand it is a constant comparison between the wise man and the fool. In God's eyes, the wise man is the one who knows what to say, when to say it, how to say it, and who to say it to. On the other hand, the fool is the one who can't manage his mouth and control his conversation. The fool constantly gives the devil free ammunition to use against him, all because he doesn't know the value of silence, or the value of thinking before speaking.

A portion of Ecclesiastes 5:6 says this: *"do not let **your mouth** cause your flesh to sin."* This goes right along with what James 3:2 declares: *"For we all stumble in many things. If anyone does **not stumble in word**, he is a perfect man, able also to bridle the whole body."* Anyone having problems controlling their carnal desires will need to address the issue of verbal mismanagement if they're ever to set themselves free from conversational self-destruction. God has entrusted us with the power to create or destroy with words. This is what puts us in the highest class of created beings, which is just a little lower than the Godhead itself.

*What is man that You are mindful of him, And the son of man that You visit him? For You have made him a **little lower than the angels**. And You have crowned him with glory and honor.*

—Psalm 8:4-5

The word translated "angels" in this verse is actually the Hebrew word *Elohim*, which is the word used for the Godhead. In short, the translators lost their nerve, so they replaced that word with one that speaks of angels, rather than the Trinity. *Young's Literal Translation* bears this out.

> "What [is] man that Thou rememberest him? The son of man that Thou inspectest him? And causest him **to lack a little of Godhead**, and with honour and majesty compassest him."
>
> —Psalm 8:4-5 YLT

Don't confuse this passage in Psalms with the passage found in Hebrews 2:5-9. They speak of two different scenarios. The verses in Hebrews 2:5-9 quote this passage in Psalms, and accurately change the word "Elohim" for the word "angels," because the context of those verses speaks of a temporary position that Jesus voluntarily accepted in order to purchase our salvation. But the verse in Psalms is different. The context of that verse is talking about God's original plan for man in creation, not redemption. From the beginning, God intended to give us the same kind of verbal power that He has.

All other created species on earth can communicate with each other, but not with words. They do so with sounds, scent, and mannerisms, but we humans are unique. We're spirits living in bodies. We think. We choose. We speak. Animals can't do that. Birds can't do that. Fish can't do that. Insects can't do that. We're the only ones who can create with words. Of course, we don't have the ability to create a universe like God, because He's God and we're not. But we are made in His image and likeness (Genesis 1:26-28). So even though we can't create to the degree that God does, we can (and should) create our *personal* universe, and that's what we've been entrusted with verbal power to do. Our words enable God to be great in our lives, or they enable the devil to steal, kill, and destroy in our lives. The words we speak determine which way things go in life now, and in eternity to come.

*And for me, that utterance may be given to me, that I may **open my mouth boldly** to make known the mystery of the gospel, for which I am an ambassador in chains; that in it I may **speak boldly, as I ought to speak**.*

—Ephesians 6:19-20

When the Apostle Paul wrote the closing remarks in his letter to the Ephesian church, he included an appeal for prayer support. What did he want them to pray about? *Bold, fearless preaching and teaching!* That same need in prayer has never changed. We need to be praying for each other, that our words are spoken and delivered with great boldness, as they should be.

BE A JESUS TO THE WORLD

Our enemies need to see and hear our boldness in Christ. When the devil steps up and tries to use his religious or secular puppets to shut us down, we need to remember that we've been entrusted with the words of eternal life (John 6:68). God is depending on us to be faithful to the call and command of the Great Commission (Mark 16:15-18). We must never allow the pressure of the world to negatively affect our message to the world. The Word of God is truth (John 17:17), and it must be proclaimed without compromise or apology, regardless of the consequences to us when we do. All of Acts Chapters 3 and 4 is an example of this. When Peter and John were used by the Lord Jesus to bring a miracle healing to the crippled man at the Beautiful Temple Gate, they were arrested and thrown in jail. They were then brought before an inquisition put together by the religious puppets to interrogate and punish these men for what they did.

And when they had set them in the midst, they asked, "By what power or by what name have you done this?" Then Peter, filled with the Holy Spirit, said to them, "Rulers of the people and elders of Israel: if we this day are judged for a good deed done to a helpless man, by what means he has been made well, let it be known to you all, and to all the people of Israel, **that by the name of Jesus Christ of Nazareth, who you crucified, who God raised from the dead, by Him this man stands here before you whole.** *This is the 'stone, which was rejected by you builders, which has become the chief cornerstone.' Nor is there salvation in any other, for there is no other name under heaven given among men by which we must be saved."*

—Acts 4:7-12

Peter made these fearless declarations. This is the same man who had denied Jesus three times prior to our Lord's crucifixion, and after the crucifixion, was hiding with the rest of the apostles for fear of the Jews (John 20:19). But now he's been saved and Spirit-filled, unafraid to speak the truth without hesitation or apology.

When Peter replied to them the way he did, they marveled not just at what he said, but by the way he said what he said. He boldly got "right up in their faces" as we say, and confronted their hypocrisies. They were told they had just rejected and murdered their Messiah by way of the cross. And then to let them have it with "both barrels," he told them the name of Jesus was the only way a person could ever be saved. Look at the reaction from the religious puppets.

Now when they **saw the boldness** *of Peter and John, and perceived that they were uneducated and untrained men, they marveled.* **And they realized that they had been with Jesus.**

—Acts 4:13

Entrusted for Eternity

Whether we speak with words of kindness and empathy, or with words of boldness and indignation, we have been entrusted to talk the talk just like Jesus did. Like Paul, we can change our approach to people, depending upon who it is we're talking to (1 Corinthains 9:19-23). But the fact remains that we have been entrusted with verbal power, so we should never hesitate to boldly proclaim the truth over our own lives first, and then to the world we are sent to in the name of Jesus.

CHAPTER 13

ENTRUSTED WITH AUTHORITY

And He said to them, **"Go into all the world and preach the gospel** *to every creature. He who believes and is baptized will be saved; but he who does not believe will be condemned. And these signs will follow those who believe:* **in My name** *they will cast out demons; they will speak with new tongues; they will take up serpents; and if they drink anything deadly, it will by no means hurt them; they will lay hands on the sick, and they will recover.*

—Mark 16:15-18

And Jesus came and spoke to them, saying. **"All authority** *has been given to Me in heaven and on earth.* **Go therefore and make disciples** *of all the nations, baptizing them in the name of the Father and of the Son and of the Holy spirit,* **teaching them** *to observe all things that I have commanded*

*you; and lo, I am with you always, even to the end of the age."
Amen.*

—Matthew 28:18-20

Notice the difference between these two sets of commands. Mark's gospel addresses the command to *preach* the gospel everywhere in all the world. Matthew's gospel addresses the command to *teach* the Christians, so they become true disciples of Christ through obedience to other commands now found in the New Testament. We preach to sinners to get them saved, then we teach these new believers to eliminate biblical ignorance regarding who they are and what they can do in Christ (Hosea 4:6). And then a third command we must follow is the need to warn people of the consequences for failing to receive God's gift of salvation:

> *Him we preach, **warning every man** and teaching every man in all wisdom, that we may present every man perfect in Christ Jesus. To this end I also labor, striving according to His working which works in me mightily.*
>
> —Colossians 1:28-29

We have been entrusted with divine authority for preaching, teaching and warning people in the name of Jesus, as soldiers in the army of the Lord (2 Timothy 2:2-4). It's vital that we understand that Jesus Christ has delegated all authority on earth to the Church, which every Christian is a part of. God the Father gave *all authority* on earth to Jesus, who then turned and transferred that mantle of authority to the Church, which is the Body of Christ. Therefore, He can only work *through the Church* because He has entrusted us with all the authority to use His name.

ENTRUSTED WITH AUTHORITY

When Jesus went back to heaven after His resurrection from the dead, Ephesians 1:21 tells us that He was seated at God's right hand, *far above* all principalities, power, might, and dominion, and every name that is named. That's awesome, but it gets better! Look at what we find from Philippians:

> Therefore God has highly exalted Him and given Him **the name which is above every name**, that at the name of Jesus **every knee should bow**, of those in heaven, and of those on earth, and of those under the earth, and that **every tongue should confess** that Jesus Christ is Lord, to the glory of God the Father.
>
> —Philippians 2:9-11

WE HAVE AUTHORITY TO USE HIS NAME

Immediately after Jesus left earth and sat down in heaven, we see the early church stepping out with its newfound authority to use the name of Jesus to confirm the fact that Jesus is alive, and the same yesterday, today, and forever (Hebrews 13:8). As discussed already, Peter was used by the Lord Jesus to raise a hopelessly crippled man back to instant health. For this Peter and John were arrested and put on trial. But here we want to go back to Acts Chapter 3, to see how this miracle of healing took place.

> Now Peter and John went up together to the temple at the hour of prayer, the ninth hour. And a certain man lame from his mother's womb was carried, whom they laid daily at the gate of the temple which is called Beautiful, to ask alms from those who entered the temple, who, seeing Peter and John about to go into the temple, asked for alms. And fixing his eyes on

*him, with John, Peter said, "Look at us." So he gave them his attention, expecting to receive something from them. Then Peter said, "Silver and gold I do not have, but **what I do have I give you: In the name of Jesus Christ of Nazareth**, rise up and walk." And he took him by the right hand and lifted him up, and immediately his feet and ankle bones received strength. So he, leaping up, stood and walked and entered the temple with them—walking, leaping, and praising God.*

—Acts 3:1-8

Fresh from being filled with Holy Spirit, Peter boldly commanded this cripple to look up at them. The man was expecting a financial handout, but what he got was something far better. He got the power that instantly healed his twisted and useless legs. This miracle took place because Peter now knew he had authority from heaven to use the name of Jesus whenever it was necessary.

And isn't this exactly what Jesus promised all of us in the Great Commission of Mark 16:15-18? In verse 18, He declared that when we preach the Word of God, specific miraculous signs would follow to confirm the gospel message. He said these signs shall follow *"them that believe. . . ."* One such sign was for believers to lay hands on the sick, and the sick would recover. It's important to take note of the fact that miracles like this are promised to all believers, not just to special leaders like Peter or John. Each one of us has been entrusted with authority to use the name of Jesus on earth. Peter told the crippled man he had something to give, and it was much better than just a financial handout. We have something to give to the world, and it's the authority to terrorize and torment the forces of darkness wherever and whenever. This is what the Lord has delegated to the church, and we must embrace the great honor and responsibility that it is.

THE DEVIL IS AFRAID OF THE NAME

> *"But so that it spreads no further among the people, let us severely threaten them, that from now on* **they speak to no man in this name.**"
>
> —Acts 4:17

Religions worldwide talk about God, and how to serve Him and please Him. This is by demonic design. The devil doesn't care about people who want to follow one of his religions that purport to follow and please "God." Along with many other forms of deception, religion is designed to deceive and destroy as many as possible. In fact, the lies of religion have sent more people to hell than any other form of deception out there. Serving "God" doesn't bring a person any closer to salvation than if they were to sing, *"Twinkle, Twinkle, little star, how I wonder what you are."* It's the name of Jesus that terrifies the devil. Why? Because that's the name of our Lord's humanity, and it was in His humanity that Jesus defeated the devil at the cross and resurrection. That's why God has declared the name of Jesus to be the one name above every other name—anywhere. At that name, *every knee* bows, and *every tongue* confesses that Jesus is Lord. Every means every. Every created being will bow and confess that Jesus is Who He is—Lord God and Savior of the world. Every believer will bow and declare it. Every angel will bow and declare it. Every demon and fallen angel will bow and declare it. Every lost sinner in hell will bow and declare it. And the devil himself will bow and declare it. Jesus is called the Last Adam—the One who finished the work of redemption (1 Corinthians 15:45; John 19:30).

The devil isn't afraid of us—but he's terrified of the name of Jesus which we have authority to use. That's why the religious puppets who were trying to stop Peter and John threatened them the way they did.

They hated the name of Jesus so much they couldn't even say it when commanding the two apostles to stop their public preaching. *"Don't you dare speak to anyone anymore in that name!"* Do you want to torment the devil? Start living according to Colossians Chapter 3:

And whatever you do in word or deed, do all in the name of the Lord Jesus, giving thanks to God the Father through Him.

—Colossians 3:17

It's not a magic charm we can flippantly speak forth like some kind of nursery rhyme. It's the highest, most powerful name in existence, and we've been entrusted with it! We must all remember that and cherish this great responsibility. Demons flee at the mention of His name.

CHAPTER 14

ENTRUSTED WITH WEAPONS OF WAR

When people join the military, they are issued uniforms and weapons. And then they're taught and trained to use those weapons efficiently and effectively. God has done the same thing with His army, the Body of Christ. He has entrusted us with powerful weapons to use that unbelievers have no access to. When Satan comes against unbelievers to steal, kill, and destroy, there is nothing they can do to defend themselves (John 10:10). But for the Christian, the Lord has given us everything we need to be victorious in spiritual combat against the devil and his demon forces. First, we have the Holy Spirit living in us (John 14:16-17). Next, He's given us the name above every name, which is the name of Jesus. After that, He's provided us with angelic assistance whenever needed (Hebrews 1:13-14). And then of course, we have God's holy Word, to instruct, guide, strengthen, and correct us. And within the Word of God, we find specific weapons specifically designed to give us the ability to fight the good fight of faith (1 Timothy 6:12).

SEVEN WEAPONS

Ephesians Chapter 6 will list for us 7 spiritual weapons we need to know how to use as we navigate life on earth for the Lord Jesus.

> *Finally, my brethren, be strong in the Lord and in the power of His might.* ***Put on the whole armor of God****, that you may be able to stand against the wiles of the devil. For we do not wrestle against flesh and blood, but against principalities, against powers, against the rulers of the darkness of this age, against spiritual hosts of wickedness in the heavenly places. Therefore* ***take up the whole armor of God****, that you may be able to withstand in the evil day, and having done all, to stand.*
>
> —Ephesians 6:10-13

So from this passage, we see several things. We see that we must be strong in the Lord. We see that we must wear all of God's armor to successfully stand against the strategies of the enemy. We see that our real enemies are spirits, not the people they control. We see that when we do take up all of God's armor, we can keep on standing as long as necessary to win these fights of faith. And as we continue reading, we see what kind of weapons we have to put on and use in spiritual combat.

> *Stand therefore, having* ***girded your waist with truth****, having put on the* ***breastplate of righteousness****, and having shod your feet with the preparation of* ***the gospel of peace****; above all, taking* ***the shield of faith*** *with which you will be able to quench all the fiery darts of the wicked one. And take* ***the helmet of salvation****, and the sword of the Spirit, which is* ***the Word of God; praying always with all prayer*** *and supplication in the Spirit. . . .*
>
> —Ephesians 6:14-18

Many books have been written, and many sermons given, which go into detailed teaching on each of these 7 weapons, but that is not the main purpose of *this book*, so here we'll just touch on the main points for each, and let the Holy Spirit amplify these things to you as He sees fit.

1. Waist girded with truth. This weapon protects the mid-section of our body, where God specifically gives us the ability to be "fruitful and multiply" (Genesis 1:22). The original KJV translation uses the word "loins" rather than "waist." Spiritually, this refers to our ability to replicate ourselves by teaching the Word of God, which is truth (John 17:17), to those we are led to teach and disciple (2 Timothy 2:2).

2. Breastplate of righteousness. This weapon protects our heart and lungs. Spiritually speaking, the righteousness of God has been imparted to us by way of the new birth. Because of that, God sees us as pure vessels, without spot, blemish, wrinkle, or sin. Second Corinthians 5:21 tells us that in Christ, we have become the righteousness of God. Not by our works, but by the work of Jesus on the cross. This means we can come boldly to God anytime, because we now have "right standing" with Him (Hebrews 4:14-16).

3. Feet covered with the gospel of peace. This weapon protects us as we travel the globe in the name of Jesus, fulfilling the Great Commissions of Mark 16:15-18 and Matthew 28:18-20. The reference to feet indicates travel, going into all the world as Jesus commanded. The gospel is called a gospel of peace, not condemnation. That is an important point never to be forgotten. Above all else, our job is to bring God's peace to all those who don't have it. Jesus left us His peace and expects us to share it with the world. The gospel is all about finding the peace that the world cannot give (John 14:27). Of course, we need to warn people about the consequences of sin (Colossians 1:28). But those warnings need to be shared in the general context of the full gospel—not just that part. (For detailed teaching on this important subject, refer to my book entitled *Divine Peace. The world didn't give it and the world can't take it away.*)

4. Shield of Faith. This is the weapon, above all others, that helps us prevail against any and all enemy attacks. The Bible describes the devil's tactics launched against us as "fiery darts." That means they are designed to inflict as much pain as quickly as possible, until we've been either totally neutralized as a Christian soldier in this life, or dead and in heaven, no longer a threat to the kingdom of darkness.

5. The Helmet of Salvation. This is the weapon that keeps our eyes on the horizon, looking ahead rather than looking behind. This helmet is also called the hope of our salvation (1 Thessalonians 5:8). Hope always deals with the future, never the past or present. Wearing this helmet gives us the ability to see beyond the present set of circumstances and embrace those exceeding great and precious promises from God (2 Peter 1:4). And how should we embrace them? By using the shield of faith, of course! This was one of Paul's go-to weapons whenever he was tempted to quit or be discouraged (Philippians 3:12-14).

6. The Sword of the Spirit. Like weapon number 1, this weapon is specifically identified as being the Word of God, but there is a difference. As we've already seen, weapon number 1 deals with the protection of our loins, or our ability to go teach and reproduce ourselves person by person. It is defensive in nature. In fact, weapons 1 through 5 are all defensive in nature, protecting and defending us from enemy attacks. However, weapon number 6 is offensive in nature. Of course, it can and should be used to defend against the lies of the devil, as Jesus did when He was tempted (Matthew 4:1-10). But in obedience to the Great Commissions of Mark 16:15-18 and Matthew 28:18-20, this is our attack weapon! Speaking God's Word releases God's power and puts our faith to work. Remember: the devil isn't afraid of us, but he's terrified of the Word of God flowing through us.

7. Praying always with all prayer. Like the Word of God, this weapon is both offensive and defensive in nature. We can pray our way through any attack brought against us by the devil, or we can pray and aggressively take ground and rescue the lost in the name of Jesus. Either way, we must develop our prayer life! Without it, our walk with God will be severely limited. The words "all prayer" indicate there are a number of prayers we need to know about, and to know which prayer is appropriate to pray at any given time. That's why the Bible says we should *study* to show ourselves approved (2 Timothy 2:15 KJV)!

CHARACTERISTICS OF OUR WEAPONRY

> For though we walk in the flesh, we do not war according to the flesh. For the weapons of our warfare **are not carnal but mighty in God for pulling down strongholds,** casting down arguments and every high thing that exalts itself against the knowledge of God, bringing every thought into captivity to the obedience of Christ, and being ready to punish all disobedience when your obedience is fulfilled.
> —2 Corinthians 10:3-5

The weapons of war we've been issued are spiritual, not carnal. We found this out from what Paul told us in Ephesians 6:12, and what he's telling the Corinthians here. You can't fight the enemy in the natural. It's a waste of time and energy and is doomed to defeat. Only by keeping our battle in the spirit realm using spiritual weapons can we be consistently victorious. All of God's weapons we've been entrusted with have 5 main characteristics:

1. Our weapons of war are spiritual, not carnal. To defeat spiritual enemies we must use spiritual weapons.

2. Our weapons are mighty in God! The Bible says Satan is shrewd (Genesis 3:1), has meticulous strategies (wiles) (Ephesians 6:11), and can disguise himself as an angel of light (2 Corinthians 11:13-14). All of that doesn't change the truth about the weapons we've been entrusted with. On our worst day, they're more than a match against the devil.

3. They are designed to pull down strongholds. The most intense battlefield takes place in our minds. Always. We must sin in our minds before we allow anything sinful to take place in the flesh. The devil knows this, and we should know it too. He seeks to establish mental strongholds, which capture and control our thinking. This leads to defeat every time, and we cannot allow that. When it comes to our thought life: *never let a foothold become a stronghold.* How do we do this? By bringing every thought into captivity to the Word of God. How do we do that? By speaking to the enemy, and to the "mountain" that we are facing. This is what Jesus taught us to do (Mark 11:22-24).

4. They are designed to cast down imaginations. The devil's first objective is to plant ideas and pictures in our minds. If the devil has *already* created a mental stronghold in a Christian's mind, these weapons of war will cast them down and cast them out. If he has been unable to neutralize the on-fire for God Christian, then he tries to slow them down to the point where they are no longer a threat to him and his kingdom. The NKJV translation in this passage uses the word "arguments," but the KJV translation uses the word "imaginations." I like that word much more. Philippians 4:8 plainly tells us what to think on. They are things that are *true, noble, just, pure, lovely, of good report, virtuous, and praiseworthy.* Nothing else! Cast down any thought that isn't in line with what the Word of God tells us to think on.

5. They are designed to protect our soul. Right now Christians live in a flesh-and-blood physical body which is not yet saved. Our born again spirit lives within this body, which Jesus called a temple made with hands (Mark 14:58). Every human spirit possesses a soul, which is what the Bible calls part of our "inner man" (Ephesians 3:16). The inner man is the spirit and soul together. The soul consists of our mind, will, and emotions. Putting the Word of God first place in our lives will enable us to seal up our mental faculties and prevent the devil from infiltrating with his never-ending attempts to create the footholds that lead to strongholds. By leaning on the Word of God, we can make the right decisions that constantly reject lies from the enemy and maintains an even-keel with our emotional state of mind.

THE COMBAT ATTITUDE

> Being **watchful** to this end with all perseverance and supplication all the saints, and as for me, that utterance may be given to me, that I may **open my mouth boldly** to make known the mystery of the gospel, for which I am an ambassador in chains; that in it **I may speak boldly**, as I ought to speak.
>
> —Ephesians 6:18b-29

Remember, we've been entrusted with free will. That means we can choose to have the right attitude about living in a world at war for the souls of men. We can be lukewarm, like many are today inside the Body of Christ (Revelation 3:15-16). Or we can be zealous and "on fire" for the Lord (Numbers 14:24; John 2:17). There are two ways to display combat readiness.

1. Vigilance. Our responsibility in spiritual warfare is to constantly monitor enemy activity in our lives, or in the lives of those close to us. Being watchful means being vigilant and alert, and not allowing the enemy to launch surprise attacks successfully. Being watchful to the end is one way to demonstrate the kind of attitude God loves and is prepared to bless.

2. Boldness. We are not supposed to tiptoe through the tulips, hoping nobody gets offended with who we are and what we have to say. Hardly! To the contrary, we're to "push the envelope" as they say, and aggressively move out into the kingdom of darkness with the armor of light (Romans 13:12). If people hate us for it, so what! Jesus told us to expect resistance and persecution, as it is right now for millions of saints laboring for God in hostile countries and areas of the world (John 15:20).

THE FIGHT GOES ON

> *Deliver me, O Lord, from evil men; preserve me from violent men, who plan evil things in their hearts; they **continually** gather together for war. They sharpen their tongues like a serpent; the poison of asps is under their lips. Keep me, O Lord, from the hands of the wicked; preserve me from violent men, who have **purposed** to make my steps stumble. The proud have hidden a **snare for me, and cords**; they have **spread a net** by the wayside; they have **set traps** for me. I said to the Lord: "You are my God; hear the voice of my supplications, O Lord. O God the Lord, the strength of my salvation You have covered my head in the day of battle. Do not grant O Lord, the desires of the wicked; do not further his wicked scheme, lest they be exalted.*
>
> —Psalm 140:1-8

Our enemies *continually* gather together for war against us. Notice there are four ways the devil comes against us. He uses *snares, cords, nets, and traps.* That means the way he attacks you might not be the way he attacks me. One way or another, he's coming to take us out! Never forget this. When Jesus comes back at the end of the tribulation, Satan and his ilk will disappear from the earth (Revelation 20:1-3), but 1,000 years later, he'll be loosed and allowed to tempt and deceive those born during the Millennium who have never had to choose between good and evil. He can't help it—that is his twisted and evil nature! And then finally, after the Great White Throne judgment, the devil and every spirit that ever followed him will be thrown into the lake of fire forever (Revelation 20:7-14).

BE STRONG AND STAY STRONG

> *And now, behold, the Lord has kept me alive, as He said, these forty-five years, ever since the Lord spoke this word to Moses while Israel wandered in the wilderness; and now, here I am this day, eighty-five years old. As yet I am **as strong this day as on the day that Moses sent me**; just as my strength was then, so now is my **strength for war**, both for going out and for coming in.*
>
> —Joshua 14:10-13

Satan will *never* stop looking for ways to steal, kill, and destroy us. He hates everyone, saved or unsaved, but he especially hates Christians. That being said, we must be strong and stay strong. We need to get there and stay there. Why? *For the war effort!* We're entrusted with all these weapons, for the express purpose of being strong enough to effectively *do something* meaningful in the world-wide thrust for souls. We must prevail! There's no other alternative for a believer.

DON'T GET ENTANGLED

*No one engaged in warfare **entangles himself** with the affairs of this life, that he may please him who enlisted him as a soldier.*

—2 Timothy 2:3-4

Finally, being entrusted with weapons of war means we avoid becoming entangled in the affairs of life. The devil doesn't entangle us—we entangle ourselves. Soldiers of Christ must never let this happen. (My first book, BE STRONG STAY STRONG, was written specifically addressing this subject. I strongly recommend you get it and read it).

CHAPTER 15

ENTRUSTED WITH LIFE

*So God created man in His own image; in the image of God He created him; male and female He created them. Then God blessed them, and God said to them "**Be fruitful and multiply**, fill the earth and subdue it. . . ."*

—Genesis 1:27-28

When I was writing this manuscript, this chapter was not originally in my notes. As I was moving through my outlines and my thoughts, God stepped in and let me know He wanted this chapter included in the book. This took place in my hotel room, hundreds of miles away from home, preparing for a service later that day. I was sitting up in bed, talking to the Lord about many things, and looking across the room at my computer, which had been left open overnight. On the home screen was a picture of Tristan Rei Keyes, our first grandson, when he was about 3 months old. While his mother was playing with him, dad took video and pictures. The one I had on my computer screen was a still shot of him laughing, with his eyes closed, obviously enjoying the love he was receiving at the moment. That photo had been on my home screen for several weeks, and I had always enjoyed just looking at it throughout the day. But on this particular morning, as I thought about this book I was writing, I heard myself say out loud: *we've been entrusted with life!*

Sometimes the awesomeness of that statement is lost in the day-to-day life we live. Babies are conceived and delivered every day, all over the world. But how many times do we ever stop and really think about what a privilege and honor it is to actually replicate life itself! Of course we know that God is the Father of spirits (Hebrews 12:9), but He has given each human being the ability to actually partner with Him in the creation of life, because we are all spirits *living in physical bodies*. When He told Adam and Eve to be fruitful and multiply, He was enabling and authorizing us to join Him in the act of creating a complete human being—from scratch, as we say. The moment a man's sperm unites with a woman's egg, God's Word explodes inside the womb of that woman, and eternal life is created. A human spirit that never existed before is now alive, and the nine-month process of pregnancy begins, which enables that little human spirit to be born into this physical world with the body prepared for it. Jesus even talked about this in His own prayers to His Father God.

> *Therefore, when He came into the world, He said "Sacrifice and offering You did not desire,* **but a body You have prepared for Me.***"*
>
> —Hebrews 10:5

How did God prepare a body for Jesus? Through the miraculous work of the Holy Spirit. A virgin shall conceive, and give birth (Isaiah 7:14). The second person of the Trinity left heaven and came to earth as a man, in the same way every human comes into the world. There was the miraculous conception, then Mary's pregnancy, and finally, our Lord's birth. But what about those first few years after the birth? God was watching over Jesus of course, but who took care of Him in the natural? Who fed Him? Who bathed Him? Who did what every mother does in nursing, caring, and loving her child? And what about Joseph? Nobody writes books about Joseph, but without his leadership as the "father" in this family, what would have been the outcome? He was obedient to respond to several dreams God gave him for protection of his wife and infant child, even though I'm sure he struggled to understand this whole event! If you go back and read, when Mary told him that she was pregnant, and when the towns folk realized she was pregnant, he was mindful to put her away secretly. He was a good man who was trying to understand while Mary kept telling him she was still a virgin and had kept herself pure for him, even though she was obviously pregnant! Put yourself in his shoes and try to appreciate how necessary it was for him to trust God and follow instructions to the letter, all of it purely by faith.

The takeaway from all of that is enormous! Until Jesus was old enough to fend for Himself, Joseph and Mary were the ones entrusted with His care, in every way a father and mother is responsible to care for and protect their children. Think about it! Along with God the Father and the Holy Spirit, Jesus is the Creator of all substance and life, both in the spirit world and this world (Colossians 1:16). And yet, He still came to earth the same way we all do (except for Adam and Eve), and was subservient to his earthly guardians in every way (Luke 2:51). And his earthly "parents" were charged by God to take care of the *Savior of the human race*, until such time as Jesus reached a place in this life where He could take care of Himself, and continue preparing for His three-year earthly assignment to save us all from our sins. The whole thing is beyond our ability to comprehend, it's so wonderful and amazing!

But when you're praising God for all of it, don't forget to appreciate the family dynamic that was in play.

ENTRUSTED TO PROTECT LIFE

Every child born into this world deserves to be loved and cared for. They never asked to be born—that decision was made by the parents when they decided to "multiply." And it doesn't matter *where* they were born. God still expects us all to love and care for life—to the best of our ability. When you get right down to it, having the power to create life—and then protect it once introduced into this world—is one of the greatest honors and responsibilities we could ever have, if not the greatest. God creates the human spirit, but He waits until *we decide* to join together sexually to create the temple that this little spirit from God will live in all the days of its life.

I know in my own life as a father to our two children, there were choices I made or things I did that weren't always right in God's eyes. I could've been a better father to them at times, but I know God knows I loved them with my whole heart, and love them more now than ever. And they know it too, because I've told them as often as I can, and do my best to show them every day. None of us, as parents, can ever go back and fix the mistakes we made when we were younger and inexperienced with parenting. All we can do, and all we must do, is ask the Lord to forgive us and move on. But I think the whole dynamic of being fathers and mothers starts with what this chapter addresses. God *chose* to give us the ability to replicate physical life, and to partner with Him in the work of creating an eternal human spirit that possesses a soul (1 Thessalonians 5:23).

> *Then they brought little children to Him, that He might touch them; but the disciples rebuked those who brought them. But when Jesus saw it, He was **greatly displeased** and said to*

them, "Let the little children come to Me, and do not forbid them; for of such is the kingdom of God.

—Mark 10:13-14

Jesus rebuked His disciples for not appreciating the little ones as He did. We have the been entrusted with this God-given ability to create the bodies they live in, made in the image and likeness of God Himself. "Behold, children are a heritage from the Lord, the **fruit of the womb is a reward**. Like arrows in the hand of a warrior, so are the children of one's youth. Happy is the man who has his quiver full of them; they shall not be ashamed, but shall speak with their enemies in the gate," (Psalm 127:3-5). Creating and giving birth to our children is called a *reward* from God! Think about that! We can actually cooperate with God Himself in creating someone whom God can love, and whom we can love—forever! Angels weren't created this way. As far as we know, God just created them all at once, with the power that only He possesses. But for us, He wanted us to share in the joy of creation, and then the joy of molding these little warriors into men and women that will serve God, and be loved by God—forever. Amazing!

ENTRUSTED TO DEVELOP AND TRAIN

Train up a child in the way he should go, and when he is old he will not depart from it.

—Proverbs 22:6.

We have not just been entrusted with the conception of physical life itself, but also with the responsibility to watch over our babies as they become young children, then teenage youth, and then full-grown adults. As I sat in that bed looking over at little Tristan's sweet, pure, and innocent smile, it was a reminder that in God's eyes, we will answer someday for the way we responded and carried out this awesome responsibility, privilege and honor. Those words in Proverbs are the words every parent will be held responsible for when they stand before God someday in heaven

When we meditate on these things, it becomes obvious why the devil prioritizes the destruction of the family unit, as designed by God. It starts with the sin of sex outside of marriage, then the lack of awareness regarding the marriage relationship itself, moving into all the different expressions of perversity we see today in society. Once we throw off all spiritual and scriptural restraints and let our unregenerate flesh control our appetites, we're on the road to destruction and death in every way possible. Paul addresses this in his letter to the Romans.

> *Therefore God also gave them up to uncleanness, in the lusts of their hearts, to dishonor their bodies among themselves, who exchanged the truth of God for the lie, and worshiped and served the creature rather than the Creator, who is blessed forever. Amen. For this reason God gave them up to vile passions. For even their women exchanged the natural use for what is against nature. Likewise also the men, leaving the natural use of the woman, burned in their lust for one another, men with men committing what is shameful, and receiving in themselves the penalty of their error which was due.* ***And even as they did not like to retain God in their knowledge, God gave them over to a debased mind, to do those things which are not fitting.***
>
> —Romans 1:24-28

That's just a small excerpt from Romans Chapter 1. Read Chapters 1 and 2 in their entirety. The whole reason for the current disintegration of our society starts in the area of sexual disobedience and sinful perversion. This is all the more reason to cherish and appreciate the fact that God chose to entrust us with the responsibility and honor to conceive and then raise our children in the nurture and admonition of the Lord.

STANDING FOR RIGHTEOUSNESS PUBLICLY

Being entrusted as bondservants of the Lord also means we do our part in protecting and maintaining the law and order that God ordains in nations as a whole. Many believers believe the Church shouldn't be involved in civic matters, and specifically, in matters of state, quoting verses such as Romans 13:1-2.

> Let every soul be subject to the governing authorities. For there is no authority except from God, and the authorities that exist **are appointed by God**. Therefore whoever resists the authority resists the ordinance of God, and those who resist will bring judgment on themselves.
>
> —Romans 13:1-2

But keep reading! Don't stop after verse 2. Quote the verses that follow.

> For rulers are not a terror to good works, but to evil. Do you want to be unafraid of the authority? Do what is good, and you will have praise from the same. For he is God's minister to **you for good**. But if you do evil, be afraid; for he does not bear the sword in vain; for he is God's ministers, an avenger to execute wrath **on him who practices evil**.
>
> —Romans 13:3-4

Without going into extensive detail, this passage, as well as others, clearly tells Christians to objectively analyze the behavior and activities of those in civic authority, and with their votes, support those who do good according to God's Word, and reject those who don't. Simple. In the countries with political parties that vie for elected positions of authority, don't just listen to what they say. *Look at what they do, and see if it lines up with the Word of God.* Take time to look at their political party's platform, which states what they believe and will try to implement if elected. When you compare that to God's Word, the choices about who to vote for becomes very clear.

In the United States, as an example, there are 2 political parties. One of them has publicly declared a platform diametrically opposed to everything God stands for in His Word—*everything*. Starting with the sanctity of life before birth, they are actively working to encourage the murder of innocent, helpless infants before birth, and even after birth—all under the misguided, selfish concept of "choice." But that's only the tip of their iceberg of filth. They are actively attempting to destroy our country from within, and replace our system of government with another system which has been responsible for the death and slaughter of *millions of* people historically—just in the last 100 years or so. Christians who understand the honor and responsibility of being entrusted with the gospel should NEVER vote for candidates from a party like that. Never. And yet, there are multitudes of professing Christians who do exactly that—in every election. I believe they will answer for this on judgment day, and it isn't going to be pretty. A vote for someone and the party they are a part of is to endorse what they say and do. That makes them complicit in the evil and ungodliness that runs rampant in the lives of the citizenry. Period.

Being entrusted with life also means we exercise civic duties in a way that exemplifies our commitment to the Lord and all that He holds dear. This is also why the devil works so hard to use his puppets in government, social media, academia, entertainment, and medicine to celebrate and protect the "right" to murder unborn children in their mother's womb. When we talk about these things, I hasten to remind everyone that abortion is *not* the unpardonable sin. There is forgiveness for that sin just like there is for any other sin. Children who are aborted prior to birth are taken to heaven, and there they are nurtured and trained. Many people who have gone to heaven and come back attest to this fact. Aborted babies are not destroyed. They are just transferred to heaven to be loved and cared for there. If mothers who do this to their unborn child repent and ask the Lord for forgiveness, they get it—immediately. Of course, there are emotional scars and remorse that must be dealt with, but here again, we see a loving and caring Savior, who is easily touched with the feeling of our weaknesses and infirmities (Hebrews 4:15). He will always be there to walk us through the process of emotional healing that needs to take place whenever people turn away from sins like this.

But on the other hand, those poor souls out there who are rabid promoters of abortion "rights," their day in court is coming, and I shudder to think what it will be like for them at the Great White Throne Judgment (Revelation 20:11). They can scream all they want, rant and rave about "my body my choice," and all of that ignorant and pathetic garbage, but they'll stand in judgment someday in heaven, and they won't have the banners that they waved at their "rally," and they won't have the protection of a warped, twisted, and bribed assembly of ungodly politicians, doctors, educators, bloggers, and entertainers. They are working overtime to misuse and misapply the "hate" issue. These fools will find out one day what God hates, and for them, judgment will be as severe as it will be justified.

The scriptures are clear. Abortion is murder, period. It is the slaughtering of a helpless and defenseless human being. Every doctor that does the cutting, sucking, and dismembering, along with every assistant in that room or clinic, and every mother that consents to this will stand in judgment for it in heaven. And every slaughtered baby that had their life taken from them by these people will stand at the judgment to point their fingers at those who murdered them. *Unless*—true repentance is experienced, and those sins washed away in this life before physical death closes the day to free will choice. There are exceptions to this, of course. If a woman is forced to have this procedure done against their will, or their life is in jeopardy during the pregnancy or birth attempt, they'll not be held responsible for it on judgment day. As long as a person has breath in their lungs and the power to choose, all sins of this nature can be forever forgiven. I emphasize this to anyone who made such decisions that resulted in the taking of an innocent baby's life. *You can be forgiven!* You can have those sins washed away forever by the blood of the Lamb. You can look forward to seeing that precious little one someday soon in heaven, and be with them forever in the presence of the Lord. I don't apologize for saying these things. It's the truth, and if people get mad, too bad for them! Just like what Paul said to his persecutors in Acts.

> Then Paul and Barnabas **grew bold and said**, "It was necessary that the Word of God should be spoken to you first, but since you reject it, and **judge yourselves unworthy of everlasting life**, behold, we turn to the Gentiles.
>
> —Acts 13:46

> But when they opposed him and blasphemed, he shook his garments and said to them, "**your blood be upon your own heads; I am clean**. From now on I will go to the Gentiles.
>
> —Acts 18:6

CHAPTER 16

ENTRUSTED WITH PURPOSE

Therefore, when He came into the world, He said: "Sacrifice and offering you did not desire, but a body You have prepared for Me. In burnt offerings and sacrifices for sin You had no pleasure. Then I said, Behold, **I have come**—*in the volume of the book it is written of Me—***to do Your will, O God***."*

—Hebrews 10:5-10

From His birth until His death and resurrection, Jesus was aware of God's purpose for His life. He wasn't wasting time searching for some meaningful pursuit. From the Word of God, we know that as early as the age of twelve, He was fully aware of His purpose, which He clearly stated to Joseph and Mary when they found Him in the temple discussing doctrine with the Jewish leadership. *"And He said to them, 'Why did you seek Me? Did you not know that I must be about My Father's business?'"* (Luke 2:49). Having that awareness gave our Lord the strength to weather all the persecution and hatred the devil's puppets threw against Him. As we found out in Chapter 8, Jesus was lean, mean, and clean. He knew His purpose was to know and fulfill God's perfect will for His life. It's the same for you and me today. First and foremost, we are here on earth to find, know, and do God's perfect will. Period. Everything starts from that foundation.

> Now this is the confidence that we have in Him, that **if we ask anything according to His will**, He hears us. And if we know that He hears us, **whatever we ask**, we know that **we have** the petitions that we have asked of Him.
>
> —1 John 5:14-15

God prepared a body for Jesus to use for this, and in like manner, He prepared a body for each of us for the same reason. We're entrusted with the knowledge of that truth. When Jesus conducted the first communion service just before His crucifixion, He told His disciples to do this in remembrance of Him (1 Corinthians 11:24-25). That command isn't just confined to when we take "communion" now. That command is really to be lived out every single day. We can't go back to yesterday, and tomorrow can be planned for and confessed over, but the only time we have to do God's will in real time is today. Not yesterday or tomorrow. Today. In short, we should be doing life in remembrance of Jesus—living it like Jesus lived His life—with the same awareness of God's purpose for why we were born for such a time as this (Esther 4:14).

KNOWN FROM ETERNITY PAST

> **Before** I formed you in the womb I knew you; **before** you were born I sanctified you; I ordained you a prophet to the nations.
>
> —Jeremiah 1:5

ENTRUSTED WITH PURPOSE

It's amazing to think that from eternity past, God has seen us and knows us! The Lord was making ready for our arrival, long before our parents got together in the act of marriage and conceived our earthly tent. When Mom and Dad got busy in bed, so to speak, they created our body in the physical sense, but God created our spirit which gave that body life. We are spirits with souls living in bodies (1 Thessalonians 5:23). He, and He alone, is the Father of spirits (Hebrews 12:9). And once conceived, we spent 9 months in the darkness of our mother's womb, developing and being formed for God's glory.

> *For you formed my inward parts; You covered me in my mother's womb. I will praise You, for I am fearfully and wonderfully made; marvelous are Your works, and that my soul knows very well. My frame was not hidden from You, **when I was made in secret**, and skillfully wrought in the lowest parts of the earth. Your eyes saw my substance, **being yet unformed**, and in Your book they all were written, the days fashioned for me, **when as yet there were none of them**.*
>
> —Psalm 139:13-16

In a very real sense, when we were formed in our mother's womb, God was preparing us for His purpose. He has prepared bodies for us to live in and use for His glory. As we've already stated; this is why abortion is such a horrible sin. Truly, it is murder in God's eyes because that heinous procedure destroys a life that God had a plan and purpose for.

> *I beseech you therefore, brethren, by the mercies of God, that you present your bodies a living sacrifice, holy, acceptable to God, **which is your reasonable service**. And do not be conformed to this world, but be transformed by the*

renewing of your mind, that you may prove what is that good and acceptable and **perfect will of God**.

—Romans 12:1-3

We're told to present our bodies a living sacrifice, holy and acceptable to God, which is our reasonable service! It is "reasonable" for each of us to prioritize the knowing and doing of God's perfect will—not just His permissible will. There's a big difference between those two, and we need to know that. God tolerates a lot when we live life in His permissible will, prioritizing our choices according to our desires and not His. But that attitude and lifestyle cuts God off from being the great blessing in our lives He wants to be. And according to this passage in Romans, we find that God's will for our lives can be either good, acceptable, or perfect. We should want His perfect will, nothing less! That's where we find the grace, power, and provision we need to make a real difference in this life for the Lord. This is especially true because we've been entrusted by God in so many areas, starting with the gospel itself. One of the most effective ways to pursue God's perfect will is to pray for it. Paul addressed this point in his letter to the Colossian Church, and David did the same in the Old Testament.

> For this reason we also, since the day we heard it, do not cease to pray for you, and to ask that you may be filled with the **knowledge of His will** in all wisdom and spiritual understanding.
>
> —Colossians 1:9

> Epaphras, who is one of you, a bondservant of Christ, greets you, always laboring fervently for you in prayers, that you may stand perfect and complete in **all the will of God**.
>
> —Colossians 4:12

Cause me to hear Your lovingkindness in the morning, for in You do I trust; cause me to know the way in which I should walk, for I lift up my soul to You. Deliver me, O Lord, from my enemies; in You I take shelter. **Teach me to do Your will**, *for You are my God; Your Spirit is good. Lead me in the land of uprightness.*

—Psalm 143:8-10

So, Paul prayed this kind of prayer for the Colossian brethren, and so did Epaphras. You and I should be praying that kind of prayer as well, each and every day. David's prayer specifically asks to know the way in which we should walk. Why? Because when God teaches us the importance of knowing His perfect will for our lives, we can walk out each day in sync with the Holy Spirit's plans and purposes.

PREPARING FOR HIS PURPOSE

So I said, **'What shall I do, Lord?'** *And the Lord said to me, 'Arise and go into Damascus, and there you will be told all things* **which are appointed for you to do.***'*

—Acts 22:10

In the *A.S. Worrell Translation* of this verse, the word "appointed" is changed to the word "arranged." *And I said, 'What shall I do, Lord?,' and the Lord said to me, 'Arising, go into Damascus, and there it shall be told you concerning all things which have been arranged for you to do.'* We will use that translation to discover *six things* we must do to prepare for God's purpose in life, using what Paul asked and what the Lord said in reply.

1. WHAT DO YOU WANT ME TO DO? The first question Paul asked dealt with what he should be doing. In other words, we have to want to *do* something! I'm reminded of a great story in the Old Testament that illustrates this.

> *Now there were four leprous men at the entrance of the gate; and they said to one another, "Why are we sitting her until we die? If we say, 'We will enter the city,' the famine is in the city, and we shall die there. And if we sit here, we die also. Now therefore, come, let us surrender to the army of the Syrians. If they keep us alive, we shall live; and if they kill us, we shall only die." And* **they rose at twilight** *to go to the camp of the Syrians; and when they had come to the outskirts of the Syrian camp, to their surprise no one was there. For the Lord had caused the army of the Syrians to hear the noise of chariots and the noise of horses—the noise of a great army; so they said to one another, "look, the king of Israel has hired against us the kings of the Hittites and the kings of the Egyptians to attack us?!" Therefore,* **they arose and fled at twilight**, *and left the camp intact—their tents, their horses, and their donkeys—and they fled for their lives.*
>
> —2 Kings 7:3-7

If you read on, you'll find that the four lepers eventually went and informed the king of what had happened, and when he had verified the leper's story, they plundered the belongings and possessions of the enemy in total victory. But notice carefully the timeline for what God did to deliver His people, using these four lepers. At what time did the lepers rise up to surrender to the enemy? Twilight. At what time did the enemy rise up to run for their lives? Twilight. In other words, *when the lepers did something, God did something!* Don't forget that, because that truth still applies today. When we do something in line with God's perfect will, God's does something to make sure that what He wants gets accomplished.

ENTRUSTED WITH PURPOSE

*What shall I **render to the Lord** for all His benefits toward me?*

—Psalm 116:12

We can sum up the entire plan of salvation with this truth: *God did something for us, and now we should do something for Him.* What would that "something" be? His perfect will. Getting in the game. Being a player not just a spectator. Answering like Isaiah did in Isaiah 6:8, when the Godhead was asking Each Other where They could find dependable workers to use. His answer should be the same for all of us. *Here am I Lord, send me!* Never forget: our life is never just about us. It's about partnering with the Lord to help others in His name. That's what being entrusted by God is all about.

2. ARISING! This deals with preparation prior to implementation. As much as possible, it's important to plan ahead, and make ready for divine deployment. As an example, we read all about the many accomplishments of Paul's ministry, but must understand the time taken to prepare for that.

> *But when it pleased God, who separated me from my mother's womb and called me through His grace, to reveal His Son in me, that I might preach Him among the Gentiles, I did not immediately confer with flesh and blood, nor did I go up to Jerusalem to those who were apostles before me; **but I went to Arabia**, and returned again to Damascus. Then after **three years** I went up to Jerusalem to see Peter, and remained with him fifteen days.*
>
> —Galatians 1:15-18

Notice the timeline in what Paul told the Galatians. He didn't just start out preaching like a wild man the moment the scales fell from his eyes in Judas' house (Acts 9:10-19). No, he went to Arabia. Why? To study and learn about the mystery of the gospel (Ephesians 3:3-9). Once he understood God's plan of salvation included the Gentiles as well as the Jews, he needed to know who he was anointed to be, and what his ministry was going to accomplish. That's why the Bible instructs us to *study to show ourselves approved* (2 Timothy 2:15 KJV). That's what "arising" is all about.

3. GO! Once we know what God wants us to do, we need to commit. We need to "pull the trigger," as they say. We have to be willing to *risk* whatever we have in order to obey God and step out in faith to do His perfect will. I've already mentioned Isaiah 6:8. The prophet told the Lord he was available. He said, "Here am I, send me Lord!" Most Christians reply to that question from God by saying: "There they are Lord, send them!"

> *Gather My saints together to Me, those who have made a* **covenant with Me by sacrifice***.*
>
> —Psalm 50:5

Notice that God wants to have a gathering, but He specifically identifies who He wants to gather with. Only those who have made a covenant with Him by sacrifice. This verse reveals another important truth never to forget. *God never meets us at our point of convenience. He meets us at our point of sacrifice!* God gave everything to make salvation possible for us. He sent His only begotten Son into the world to save us from our sins. Jesus sacrificed everything to make that possible. He left heaven and took upon Himself the form of a bondservant and did what had to be done (Philippians 2:5-8). Therefore, who are we to refuse to do our part now? That's selfishness in its purest form. If our level of sacrifice isn't a stretch for us, God isn't impressed with our "availability." It's as simple as that.

4. INTO DAMASCUS. When we commit to God to arise and go, we must make sure we go where He wants us to go, not where we want to go for Him! He tells us where He wants us to work and labor, not the other way around. Look at how God specifically guided Paul along these lines.

> Now when they had gone through Phrygia and the region of Galatia, they were **forbidden** by the Holy Spirit **to preach the word in Asia**. After they had come to Mysia, they tried to go into Bithynia, but the Spirit **did not permit them**. So passing by Mysia, they came down to Troas. And a vision appeared to Paul in the night. A man of Macedonia stood and pleaded with him, saying "Come over to Macedonia and help us." Now after he had seen the vision, immediately we sought to go to Macedonia, concluding that the Lord had called us to preach the gospel to them.
>
> —Acts 16:6-10

Notice that when Paul left the Galatian region, they wanted to go into Asia and continue preaching there. It says they were *forbidden* by the Holy Spirit to go there. So, they altered their route, going through Mysia on their way to Bithynia. But once again, the Holy Spirit blocked their way and did not permit them to continue. So, passing by Mysia they came to Troas, and there Paul had the vision that led he and his team to where God specifically wanted them to go, which was into Macedonia. Why? Because the Lord knew who was ripe and ready to hear the gospel, and Paul didn't. Had he gone ahead and overrode the Holy Spirit's instructions, he would've wasted time preaching in Asia, Mysia, and Bithynia. They weren't ready for him and his message.

Does that mean God didn't care about the people in those other places? Of course not! But Paul wasn't the one God anointed to go to those places. Who was? *Peter, an apostle of Jesus Christ, to the pilgrims of the dispersion in Pontus, Galatia, Cappadocia, Asia, and Bithynia* (1 Peter 1:1). Paul wasn't called at that time to go into Asia, but Peter was. Paul wasn't called at that time to go into Bithynia, but Peter was. This is why in many cases, well-meaning ministers and saints end up in places they're not anointed by God to be. It pays to let God do the leading!

At least Paul had enough sense to wait on God until he knew where he was supposed to be in ministry at that time. And notice at the very beginning when he started in ministry, he was told to go *into Damascus*. Not some other city or town. But to Damascus. Make sure you find your Damascus, and I'll make sure I find mine!

5. AND THERE IT SHALL BE TOLD YOU. Guidance, purpose, direction, revelation, provision, protection—all of it comes into focus when we're where we're supposed to be, doing what we're supposed to be doing for God. When we make sure we're in the right place at the right time, everything concerning our ministry will fall into place. Does that mean there won't be testing, temptations, and trials? Of course not! In fact, Satan's work to try and destroy us will only *intensify* when we find our "Damascus" and camp there in the name of Jesus. So what! If God be for us, nobody can be against us (Romans 8:31-39).

> *Therefore, sailing from Troas, we ran a straight course to Samothrace, and the next day came to Neapolis, and from there to Philippi, which is the foremost city of that part of Macedonia, a colony. And we were staying in that city for some days. And on the Sabbath day we went out of the city to the riverside, where prayer was customarily made; and we sat down and spoke to the women who met there. Now a **certain woman named Lydia** heard us. She was a seller of purple from the city of Thyatira, who worshipped God. **The Lord opened her heart** to heed the things spoken by Paul.*

And when she and her household were baptized, she begged us, saying, "If you have judged me to be faithful to the Lord, come to my house and stay." So she persuaded us.

—Acts 16:11-15

Remember where Paul ended up, after he had tried to go into Asia, Mysia, and Bithynia? Macedonia. And notice where this encounter with Lydia and her household took place. In Philippi, the largest city in Macedonia. Lydia was the first Christian convert in Europe. From there, the gospel spread north and east, into many other parts of the earth. God knew Lydia was open to hear the gospel, so He wanted Paul to be there at that time. If he had run through the Holy Spirit's roadblocks and gone ahead to Asia, Mysia, or Bithynia, no one would've been in position to share the gospel with Lydia. Paul would've been off competing with Peter for Christian converts in Bithynia, out of God's perfect will. Sorry to say, this happens all too frequently with Christian workers. Their hearts are right, but they're out of position. They never went to their "Damascus," or if they did, they left before they were supposed to.

BE IN THE RIGHT PLACE AT THE RIGHT TIME

The greatest natural miracle in the Bible is when God stopped the rotation of the earth to give Joshua extra time to finish killing off the enemies of Israel (Joshua 10:6-13). When the Word of God says the sun stood still for about a day, that simply means the earth's rotation was stopped for about 24 hours. Amazing! Well, if you read that whole account, you'll discover that at a moment's notice, in the middle of the night, Joshua and his army had to pack up and do a midnight march *uphill* to meet the enemy. It says they *ascended* from Gilgal. Because of that, they came upon the enemy *suddenly*, something the enemy never expected. During that battle, the Lord not only rained down hailstones to assist the Israelites in killing the enemy, but He also stopped the spin of the earth, in answer to Joshua's authoritative demand for more daylight to continue the battle.

The greatest natural miracle that we find in all of scripture would never have happened if Joshua and his men weren't able to march uphill all night on a moment's notice to be in position to attack the enemy. Because we're entrusted with the gospel, being in the right place at the right time is important!

6. CONCERNING ALL THINGS THAT HAVE BEEN ARRANGED FOR YOU TO DO! God will go before us, and arrange things just so Divine encounters take place the way He wants them to. The story about how Philip was used to get the gospel message to an Ethiopian Eunuch is one such example.

> Now an angel of the Lord spoke to Philip, saying, "**Arise and go** toward the south along the road which goes down from Jerusalem to Gaza." This is desert. **So he arose and went**.
>
> —Acts 8:26

I love this story! There's so much we can glean from it. We will devote more time to Philip's trip into the desert in a later chapter, but here, let's examine it from the angle of pure obedience. First, notice Philip was told to *arise and go*. Second, notice he was told *where* to arise and go. And third, notice Philip didn't wait to pray about it or wait for "confirmation" from others. He immediately got up and went. Where did he go? Into the desert. What's out there? He doesn't know, but he knows the desert itself isn't a very pleasant place to be all by yourself. But he trusts God, and is heading towards his "Damascus," even if at that point he doesn't know where that is or what it will entail.

If we keep reading, we find that there is one man from Ethiopia out in the middle of the desert, sitting in his chariot reading from the scroll of Isaiah. This man is also a very important government official in Ethiopia, in charge of all of the Queen's wealth. He had gone to Jerusalem to worship the God of Abraham, Isaac, and Jacob, and was heading home afterwards. Philip didn't know any of this when he arose and went into the desert, on the road going down from Jerusalem to Gaza.

As he travels on, he sees the man in his chariot, and when he does, the Holy Spirit tells him to run and "overtake" this chariot. Why? Because the Eunuch is reading from what we now know to be Chapter 53 of Isaiah, which is the chapter talking about Jesus being slaughtered as the Lamb of God. Now, remember that the book of Isaiah is the biggest book in the Bible. Sixty-six chapters. And isn't it amazing to see Philip arriving at the precise moment this man is reading from Chapter 53, with questions about who is being identified there? Philip hears what he's reading and asks if he understands the subject matter. From that point, the eunuch hears the gospel, gets saved, and is water baptized. Philip then disappears into thin air and finds himself in another town named Azotus. The eunuch goes on his way, and through his conversion, the entire government of Ethiopia gets to hear the gospel, because the man just happened to be the treasurer for the Queen of Ethiopia!

How do we know that? *"And behold, a man of Ethiopia, a eunuch of great authority under Candace the queen of the Ethiopians, who had charge of all her treasury, and had come to Jerusalem to worship"* (Acts 8:27). God knew this eunuch was ready to hear the gospel, and was in charge of all the Queen's treasury. Philip didn't know this, but he didn't have to know! He just needed to obey God and allow the Lord to put him in the right place at the right time. This is how the entire country of Ethiopia was opened up to the gospel, all because God arranged for one man to witness to another man in the middle of the desert at the exact time he needed to be there! Do you see how God arranged all of this to happen? The story of how Peter introduced the gospel to the Gentile world is another example of this. We detailed this encounter in chapter six, but it bears additional study here.

> *About the ninth hour of the day he saw clearly in a vision an angel of God coming in and saying to him, "Cornelius!" And when he observed him, he was afraid, and said, "What is it, Lord?" So he said to him, "Your prayers and your alms have come up for a memorial before God. Now send men to Joppa, and send for Simon whose surname is Peter. He is lodging with Simon, a tanner, whose house is by the sea.* **He will tell you what you must do.**"
>
> —Acts 10:3-6

If you keep reading, you'll find that as Cornelius sends men to Joppa to find this man Peter, he himself is experiencing a vision as he prays on Simon's rooftop. Although he doesn't understand the vision's message, he knows enough to just pray and wait for an explanation. Well, the explanation shows up at that exact moment, when Cornelious' messengers come knocking on the door, looking for him. The Holy Spirit speaks and clearly tells Peter to go with these men, doubting nothing because He was the One who sent them. Peter goes with a number of other Jewish brethren, and once they arrive, Cornelious meets them and explains all that has happened. Let's pick up the story from there.

> *As Peter was coming in, Cornelius met him and fell down at his feet and worshiped him. But Peter lifted him up, saying, "Stand up; I myself am also a man." And as he talked with him, he went in and* **found many who had come together**. *Then he said to them, "You know how unlawful it is for a Jewish man to keep company with or go to one of another nation. But God has shown me that I should not call any man common or unclean. Therefore I came without objection as*

soon as I was sent for. **I ask, then, for what reason have you sent for me?"**

So Cornelius said, "Four days ago I was fasting until this hour; and at the ninth hour I prayed in my house, and behold, a man stood before me in bright clothing, and said, 'Cornelius, your prayer has been heard, and your alms are remembered in the sight of God. Send therefore to Joppa and call Simon here, whose surname is Peter. He is lodging in the house of Simon, a tanner, by the sea. **When he comes, he will speak to you.'** *So I sent to you immediately, and you have done well to come. Now therefore,* **we are all present before God, to hear all the things commanded you by God."**

—Acts 10:25-33

Peter went on from there to share all things that God commanded him to share. The result? Cornelious and his entire household were saved—and filled with the Holy Spirit simultaneously!

While Peter was still speaking these words, the Holy Spirit fell upon all those who heard the word. And those of the circumcision who believed were astonished, as many as came with Peter, because the gift of the Holy Spirit had been poured out on the Gentiles also. For they heard them speak with tongues and magnify God. Then Peter answered, "Can anyone forbid water, that these should not be baptized who have received the Holy Spirit just as we have?" And he commanded them to be baptized in the name of the Lord. Then they asked him to stay a few days.

—Acts 10:44-48

Look at how God arranged all of this to come to pass. Simultaneous supernatural visions for two men in two locations far away from each other. Messengers being sent to arrive at the precise moment Peter is contemplating the meaning of his vision. Cornelious patiently waiting four days for Peter to arrive, assembling his whole household in anticipation of what this unknown fisherman was going to tell them. And once again, note that the angel who appeared to Cornelious could not share the gospel with the Roman soldier. He could only tell him where he was and bring him back so *he* could share the gospel. God arranges things to get people into position to share or hear the gospel. He did it back then, and He continues to do it today.

Peter's first recorded miracle is found in Acts Chapter 3. When he began to minister to the crippled beggar who was expecting some money, he said this: *"Silver and gold I do not have,* **but what I do have I give you. . . ."** (Acts 3:6). That's what it means to be entrusted with a stewardship. We've been given something to share with someone in the Name of Jesus.

THE PRIORITIES OF PURPOSE

We've seen the six things that prepare us for God's purpose to be fulfilled in our lives. Now, we need to understand the *priorities* we must set as front-line soldiers entrusted with the gospel. I have desk plaques in my office at home and at the church that reads: THE TOP PRIORITY IS TO KEEP THE TOP PRIORITY THE TOP PRIORITY. Nothing is more important on the field of spiritual battle. There are three commands that encapsule our priorities.

1. FEAR GOD AND KEEP HIS COMMANDMENTS. Solomon wrote the Book of Proverbs and the Book of Ecclesiastes. Aside from Jesus Himself, he possessed more wisdom than anyone else (1 Kings

4:29). And yet, after all of his writings, and all of the things he did right and the things he did wrong, he comes to his final conclusion.

*"Let us hear **the conclusion of the whole matter:** Fear God and keep His commandments, for this is man's all,"* (Ecclesiastes 12:13). The *English Standard Version* says it this way: *"The end of the matter; all has been heard. Fear God and keep his commandments, **for this is the whole duty of man.**"* Fear God and keep His commandments. That's it. It's too simple to misunderstand. What Jesus said about this priority of purpose was even more blunt. *"If you love Me, keep My commandments"* (John 14:15). There's nowhere to go with that except to believe it and do it!

2. BE STRONG. STAY STRONG. When God called Joshua to replace Moses as leader of the nation of Israel, He gave him instructions to understand and follow. We can read about them in Joshua Chapter 1.

> No man shall be able to stand before you all the days of your life; as I was with Moses, so I will be with you. I will not leave you nor forsake you. **Be strong and of good courage**, for to this people you shall divide as an inheritance the land which I swore to their fathers to give them. **Only be strong and very courageous**, that you may observe to do according to all the law which Moses My servant commanded you; do not turn from it to the right hand or to the left, that you may prosper wherever you go. This Book of the Law shall not depart from your mouth, but you shall meditate in it day and night, that you may observe to do according to all that is written in it. For then you will make your way prosperous, and then you will have good success. **Have I not commanded you?** Be strong and of good **courage**; do not be afraid, nor be dismayed, for the Lord your God is with you wherever you go. Whoever rebels against your command and does not heed your words,

in all that you command him, shall be put to death. **Only be strong and of good courage."**

—Joshua 1:5-9,18

My very first book I wrote years ago was about this set of instructions from God. Its entitled *Be Strong Stay Strong* (order from mkmi.org directly, or go to Amazon Kindle). Four times in this one chapter, God tells Joshua to be strong and courageous. *Four times!* If God says anything four times in one exchange like this, He is emphasizing the importance of that particular point. And notice the rhetorical question from God in the midst of these instructions. *"Have I not commanded you?"* That means Joshua already knows the answer—and the answer is "yes!" This isn't a request or suggestion. It's a command. That's what the Book of Proverbs calls the conclusion of the whole matter, and the basic duty of every human being—more important than anything else. That's how Jesus said we prove we really love Him—by knowing and keeping His commandments. That's it. No wiggle-room here. Like what David told Solomon as he lay on his death bed: *"Consider now, for the Lord has chosen you to build a house for the sanctuary;* **be strong, and do it**" (1 Chronicles 28:10).

3. HELP OTHERS GET THERE AND STAY THERE. According to the Word of God, we are born again to help others get to where we are in Christ. It's not about us and what we want in life. It's about how God uses us to reach others in His Name, no matter how hard or challenging it may be. Why? Because we've been entrusted with the gospel, that's why!

A friend loves at all times, and **a brother is born for adversity**.

—Proverbs 17:17

What does it mean when the Bible tells us a brother is born for adversity? It means we live in a world run by the renegade spirit named Satan. He's the god of this world system (2 Corinthians 4:4 KJV), and as such, will try to stop us from fulfilling the Great Commission of Mark 16:15-18 and Matthew 28:18-20 anyway he can. Adversity is his middle name. We're supposed to be God's storm-troopers, who insert ourselves into times of great distress and persecution in the Name of Jesus, and tell the unsaved the good news of the gospel. So, are we born for adversity leveled against us? No! We're born again for the adversity of others—to be there in times of pressure and chaos, making sure people stay true to the Lord and never quit or go back. Paul had some harsh warnings about this to the Galatian churches.

> **Stand fast** therefore in the liberty by which Christ has made us free, and **do not be entangled again** with a yoke of bondage. Indeed I, Paul, say to you that if you become circumcised, Christ will profit you nothing. And I testify again to every man who becomes circumcised that he is a debtor to keep the whole law. You have become estranged from Christ, you who attempt to be justified by law; **you have fallen from grace**.
>
> —Galatians 5:1-4

This is the Apostle Paul stepping up to help the Galatian Christians handle the temptation and pressure to renounce Christ Jesus and go back under the law. This is the kind of adversity we're called to confront, getting right in the middle of such conflicts alongside the wavering brethren, reminding fellow believers that it pays eternal dividends to stay the course and not choose to fall away. In short, we're called to remind weak and wavering brethren that falling away is not an option. Hebrews Chapter 10 also addresses the need to remind people what will happen if they fall away under pressure. Here's some of what is said there:

> *It is a fearful thing to fall into the hands of the living God. But recall the former days in which, after you were illuminated, you **endured a great struggle with sufferings**. Therefore **do not cast away your confidence**, which has great reward. For you have need of endurance, so that after you have done the will of God, you may receive the promise: "For yet a little while, and He who is coming will come and will not tarry. Now the just shall live by faith; **but if anyone draws back, My soul has no pleasure in him**." But we are not of those who draw back to perdition, but of those who believe to the saving of the soul.*
>
> —Hebrews 10:31-32, 35-39

That's what it means when it says it is a fearful thing to fall into the hands of the living God! Our priorities of purpose must center around these three points.

THE PILLARS OF PURPOSE

In the same way there are three *priorities* of purpose, there are also three *pillars* of purpose. They represent the content of what we say when we speak to others in the Name of Jesus.

> *Him we **preach, warning** every man and **teaching** every man in all wisdom, that we may present every man perfect in Christ Jesus.*
>
> —Colossians 1:28

1. PREACHING. This is outreach evangelism to the lost. This is presenting the reality of heaven and hell, life and death, and the eternal consequences of rejecting Jesus as Lord and Savior. This is Mark 16:15-18 in operation, the "part 1" of the Great Commission. Although we can teach and warn people who aren't saved, preaching is God's primary method to present reality to the unsaved people who cross our path in life. One of the best little books we can use to supplement what we say directly to a sinner is, *How Good Is Good Enough?* by Andy Stanley. With *eternity* waiting for every single soul, saved or unsaved, the preacher *must* tell the truth about our destiny beyond the grave. Ignorance is what the devil counts on!

2. TEACHING. This is teaching and training disciples who are already born again. This is Matthew 28:18-20 in operation, the "part 2" of the Great Commission. We start by teaching believers the six elementary principles of Christ (Hebrews 5:12-14; 6:1-2). If they choke on those six principles, the Bible tells us to leave them alone and move on to others who are more receptive (2 John 1:7-11). We can love them and pray for them, but elementary principles are exactly that. They are the foundation for everything else we're going to learn in our walk with the Lord. In the natural realm, we can't teach calculus or advance physics until we learn the laws of addition, subtraction, multiplication, and division. Spiritually speaking, the same truths apply.

3. WARNING. This is letting Christians know what the penalties will be if they fall away or go back into the world. We've covered this point in detail already. Read and heed.

THE METHODS OF PURPOSE

1. PREACH THE WORD. Don't waste time with people. Yes, the Bible teaches us to be sensitive to our audience, and the circumstances of their lives. Paul talked about adjusting his "technique" of delivery, depending on who he was preaching to (1 Corinthians 9:22). But he never compromised on the *content* of his message. The same holds true for all of us today. Preach the Word of God without apology and without hesitation. *"For the Word of God is living and powerful, and sharper than any two-edged sword, piercing even to the division of soul and spirit, and of joints and marrow, and is a discerner of the thoughts and intents of the heart"* (Hebrews 4:12). The Word of God is a living thing! Think about that! It has the ability from God to enter into what the Bible calls our "inner man" (Ephesians 3:16), and spiritually address a sinner's spirit and soul. Amazing! All we have to do is open our mouths to share it.

> **Preach the word!** Be ready in season and out of season. Convince, rebuke, exhort, with all longsuffering and teaching.
>
> —2 Timothy 4:2

2. TEACH JUST MEN. Being born again is not the end of our responsibilities on earth. It's only the beginning. From the new birth, God has commanded us to teach others the things we learn and apply in our walk with God. Jesus showed us the way when He was here.

> Now it came to pass, when Jesus finished commanding His twelve disciples, that He departed from there **to teach and to preach** in their cities.
>
> —Matthew 11:1

> And when the Sabbath had come, He **began to teach** in the synagogue. And many hearing Him were astonished, saying, "Where did this Man get these things? And what wisdom is this which is given to Him, that such mighty works are performed by His hands!
>
> —Mark 6:2

> And Jesus, when He came out, saw a great multitude and was moved with compassion for them, because they were like

*sheep not having a shepherd. So He **began to teach** them many things.*

—Mark 6:34

Our ministry begins the day we accept Jesus as Lord and Savior. Teaching and preaching are two of the three methods of purpose we must apply in the Name of Jesus. We preach to sinners and we teach the believers. This is specifically what the Pharisees tried to stop right from the beginning when the saints began their worldwide outreach.

*And when they had brought them, they set them before the council. And the high priest asked them, saying, "Did we not strictly command you **not to teach in this name?** And look, you have filled Jerusalem with your doctrine, and intend to bring this Man's blood on us!"*

—Acts 5:27-28

It's true when the Bible says God's people perish for a lack of knowledge (Hosea 4:6).

*Give instruction to a wise man, and he will be still wiser; **Teach a just man**, and he will increase in learning.*

—Proverbs 9:9

3. HEAL THE SICK. Do you know that there is *only one time* in the New Testament where Christians are told to pray for the sick? It is found in the book of James.

*And the **prayer of faith will save the sick**, and the Lord will raise him up. And if he has committed sins, he will be forgiven. Confess your trespasses to one another, and **pray for one***

> **another, that you may be healed**. The effective, fervent prayer of a righteous man avails much.
>
> —James 5:15-16

In all other passages referencing ministry to sick people, we're told to *heal* the sick. Prayer is not mentioned in those instructions!

> **Heal the sick**, cleanse the lepers, raise the dead, cast out demons. Freely you have received, freely give.
>
> —Matthew 10:8

> He sent them to preach the kingdom of God and to **heal the sick**.
>
> —Luke 9:2

> And **heal the sick** there, and say to them, 'The kingdom of God has come near to you.'
>
> —Luke 10:9

In all of these passages, we see our Lord telling us to heal the sick, without specifically telling us we have to pray when we do. Why? Because the Holy Spirit wants us to know we already have the authority to use the Name of Jesus and *declare* the healing! This is one of those six elementary principles of Christ, found in Hebrews 6:1-2. Out of those six, number four is called *the doctrine of laying on of hands*. We could write a book on that subject alone! What did Jesus tell us to do when we encounter sick people in need of healing?

> And He said to them, "Go into all the world and preach the gospel to every creature. He who believes and is baptized will be saved; but he who does not believe will be condemned.

> *And these signs will follow those who believe: In My name they will cast out demons; they will speak with new tongues; they will take up serpents; and if they drink anything deadly, it will by no means hurt them;* **they will lay hands on the sick, and they will recover.***"*
>
> —Mark 15-18

I don't see any mention of prayer for the sick in these instructions, do you? That doesn't mean we shouldn't pray for the sick, because the book of James specifically says we can and should. However, we don't have to minister to the sick that way—we can clearly see the New Testament emphasis in on the exercising of our authority when we lay hands on the sick and declare their healing in Jesus' Name. We can *pray* or we can *say*, but because we've been entrusted with authority to use the Name of Jesus, we don't have to pray and ask for a healing. Just speak it forth!

PETER'S PROGRESSIVE REVELATION

Peter grew into this awareness, and we need to as well. Let's look at three instances where Peter was used by God to administer divine healing to people.

> *Then Peter said, "Silver and gold I do not have, but what I do have I give you:* **In the name of Jesus Christ of Nazareth**, *rise up and walk."*
>
> —Acts 3:6

> *There he found a certain man named Aeneas, who had been bedridden eight years and was paralyzed. And Peter said to him, "Aeneas,* **Jesus the Christ heals you***. Arise and make*

> *your bed." Then he arose immediately. So all who dwelt at Lydda and Sharon saw him and turned to the Lord.*
>
> —Acts 9:33-35

> *But Peter put them all out, and knelt down and prayed. And turning to the body he said,* **"Tabitha, arise."** *And she opened her eyes, and when she saw Peter she sat up.*
>
> —Acts 9:40

Notice how Peter's terminology changes in these three episodes, reflecting the progressive revelation he's receiving from the Holy Spirit. First, dealing with the lame man begging for money at the beautiful gate of the temple, Peter says this: *"in the Name of Jesus Christ of Nazareth, rise up and walk."* Secondly, dealing with the bedridden Aeneas, Peter says this: *"Aeneas, Jesus Christ heals you."* Finally, praying over the dead body of Tabitha, Peter says this: *"Tabitha, arise."* What's happening here? Peter is learning that in this sense, when he ministers healing to people, not only does he not have to pray about it, but he is also able to simply speak forth the healing because he knows he and Jesus are one in the spirit. *"But he who is joined to the Lord is one spirit with Him"* (1 Corinthians 6:17).

This doesn't mean we should all cease praying for the sick! This doesn't mean we should all cease including our Lord's Name when we declare healing over someone. It simply means we have *options* that the Word of God gives us. *There are* **diversities of gifts**, *but the same Spirit. There are* **differences of ministries**, *but the same Lord* (1 Corinthians 12:4-5). God entrusts us with more than one way to administer healing as Ambassadors of Christ (2 Corinthians 5:20). No matter which way we go, we just need be to be sure we make ourselves available to practice these three methods of purpose.

CHAPTER 17

ENTRUSTED TO TRUST

Cause me to hear Your lovingkindness in the morning, **for in You do I trust**; *cause me to know the way in which I should walk, for I lift up my soul to You.*

—Psalm 143:8

When we embrace the reality about being entrusted with the gospel—and all that goes with that—we come to a place where we realize we must learn to trust God every day of our lives. Why? Because once we answer God and tell Him we're available, the way the prophet did in Isaiah 6:8, we are going to find ourselves in situations and circumstances we have no ability to navigate without God's grace in response to our faith. That means we're going to have to trust God, especially when everything around us screams defeat, discouragement, and even death. And really, this is the very essence of what it means to walk by faith and not by sight (2 Corinthians 5:7). Review the few examples of faith we've examined in this book alone. Note the level of trust people exhibited in God's ability to guide, provide, and protect them as they went forth in obedience to God's leading. It must be the same for you and I today.

You will keep him in perfect peace, Whose mind is stayed on You, **Because he trusts in You.**

—Isaiah 26:3

Satan's plan is always to overwhelm our minds with thoughts designed to paralyze us with fear. The prescribed way to counter that is to cast down every imagination (thoughts) that exalts itself against the knowledge of God, which includes His assignments we're to carry out in the name of Jesus. Perfect peace is attainable, but not without a fight! The way we come to a place of useability before God is to have our minds stayed on God's Word. That produces the "perfect peace" we all must work to find and protect.

WORK TO REST

Therefore, since a promise remains of entering His rest, let us fear lest any of you seem to have come short of it. For indeed the gospel was preached to us as well as to them; but the word which they heard did not profit them, **not being mixed with faith** *in those who heard it.* **For we who have believed do enter that rest,** *as He has said: "So I swore in My wrath, 'They shall not enter My rest,'" although the works were finished from the foundation of the world.* **There remains therefore a rest for the people of God. For he who has entered His rest has himself also ceased from his works as God did from His.** *Let us therefore be diligent to enter that rest, lest anyone fall according to the same example of disobedience.*

—Hebrews 4:1-3,9-11

This passage from Hebrews Chapter 4 is a very telling revelation about the fight of faith, and how we come to a true place of rest in Him.

I also want to look at verses 9 through 11 from the *King James Version*, because I like how they present this truth: *"There remaineth therefore a rest to the people of God. For he that is entered into his rest, he also hath ceased from his own works, as God did from his.* **Let us labour therefore to enter into that rest***, lest any man fall after the same example of unbelief."*

How do we "labor to enter into God's rest?" *With trust.* The fights of faith ultimately come down to whether we trust God's Word—or not. That is the "labor." That's the battle to keep Satan's lies out of our minds and prevent them from building those footholds that he hopes with become strongholds (2 Corinthians 10:3-5). If God is going to entrust us with any level of responsibility, He is also entrusting us to trust Him to bring us through to victory every time.

> **Trust in the Lord with all your heart,** And **lean not on your own understanding**; In all your ways acknowledge Him, And He shall direct your paths.
>
> —Proverbs 3:5-6

Using my life as the example, I left the USA for the Philippines in September 1980 with a one-way plane ticket, $20 in my pocket, and only a couple hundred dollars of promised support. While still a Bible school student at Rhema, I wrote three letters to the Filipino minister God assigned me to go work for, but he never answered my letters. So, I left home with no money and no way back, not knowing if anyone even knew I was coming. To say the least, I was fighting the fear cloud all the way. But I just decided to trust God with all my heart, not leaning to my own understanding. I didn't know what was in store for me on the other side of the world, but God knew, and entrusted me with the power of choice. I chose to trust in Him. Years later, I can look back and use that example as just one of many which I have exercised in my walk of faith.

Entrusted for Eternity

The same is true for you, and for all of us. Trust God. He will never leave you or forsake you (Hebrews 13:5).

One of the most beloved passages in the Bible highlights the importance of trust.

He who dwells in the secret place of the Most High

Shall abide under the shadow of the Almighty.
I will say of the Lord, "He is my refuge and my fortress;
My God, in Him I will trust.*"*

Surely *He shall deliver you from the snare of the fowler*
And from the perilous pestilence.
He shall cover you with His feathers,
And under His wings you shall take refuge;
His truth shall be your shield and buckler.
You shall not be afraid of the terror by night,
Nor of the arrow that flies by day,
Nor of the pestilence that walks in darkness,
Nor of the destruction that lays waste at noonday.

A thousand may fall at your side,
And ten thousand at your right hand;
But it shall not come near you.
Only with your eyes shall you look,
And see the reward of the wicked.

Because you have made the Lord, who is my refuge,
Even the Most High, your dwelling place,
No evil shall befall you,
Nor shall any plague come near your dwelling;
For He shall give His angels charge over you,
To keep you in all your ways.

ENTRUSTED TO TRUST

In their hands they shall bear you up,
Lest you dash your foot against a stone.
You shall tread upon the lion and the cobra,
The young lion and the serpent you shall trample underfoot.

"Because he has set his love upon Me, therefore I will deliver him;
I will set him on high, because he has known My name.

He shall call upon Me, and I will answer him;
I will be with him in trouble;
I will deliver him and honor him.
With long life I will satisfy him,
And show him My salvation."

—Psalm 91

David knew what we need to know today. No matter what the enemy comes against us with, we can stay steady and steadfast, because we choose to trust in the Lord our God. And notice that according to verse 2, this is something that we say, not just think. And because we make up our minds to state our trust in God in the face of demonic attack, God responds and lets us know that because we trust in Him, He will do what only He can do for us. He will *deliver* him. He will *set him on high*. He will *answer* when we call upon Him for help. He will *be with him in trouble*. He will *deliver and honor* him. He will satisfy him with *long life*. And most importantly, He will show him *His salvation*. God is letting us know that trust is the outward expression of faith, and that we're entrusted with that responsibility. Trusting God opens many doors for blessings to come our way. It's not up to Him—it's always up to us.

PART THREE:

THE HONOR

CHAPTER 18

THE UNKNOWN SOMEBODY

As unknown, and yet **well known**.

—2 Corinthians 6:9

When believers truly understand the awesome honor and responsibility of being entrusted with the gospel, personal recognition and secular accolades are no longer important. Proverbs 16:18 tells us that pride goes before a fall, and the poster boy for this sin is the devil himself. The Bible says he was lifted up in pride (Ezekiel 28:17). I'm sorry to say this same sin infects and corrupts many a man or woman of God today. Make sure you're not another casualty of war because of it.

GOD SEES IN SECRET

When doing business for God, be humble and acknowledge the fact that we are what we are and do what we do by the grace of God (1 Corinthians 15:10). Acts of outreach, compassion, and kindness are never overlooked or missed by the Lord. On the other hand, every evil work or plot hatched by the ungodly is seen, heard, and recorded in heaven. Nobody gets away with anything—ever.

> *... In the day when God **will judge the secrets of men** by Jesus Christ, according to my gospel.*
>
> —Romans 2:16

No secret on earth will stay secret in heaven. Every word, every deed, and the motive of the heart when speaking and doing on earth is recorded in books in heaven. Those books will be brought before each person and analyzed against the Word of God on the day of their judgment (Matthew 12:34-37; Revelation 20:12). This is good news for believers, who sometimes get discouraged when they think nobody sees or appreciates their efforts to obey God. It's also very reassuring, knowing that vengeance belongs to God—we don't need to try and vindicate ourselves whenever we've been persecuted in some way. He'll take care of all of that at the proper time and place.

NOBODY ELSE NEEDS TO KNOW

To emphasize this point, the Bible contains many examples of people doing great things for God by simply doing what they were told to do, without anyone taking notice. Paul includes this as a descriptive characteristic of his ministry team. They were unknown but at the same time, well known. Unknown by men, but well known by God. At the end of the day, isn't that all that matters? Our lives are going to be measured and judged by God and His Word. He sees everything, so who cares if anyone down here sees or knows what we say or do in the name of Jesus? Wanting to be noticed by men is another expression of pride—no different than the pride that turned Lucifer into Satan. Jesus emphasized this in his public sermons:

THE UNKNOWN SOMEBODY

***Take heed** that you do not do your charitable deeds before men, **to be seen by them**. Otherwise you have no reward from your Father in heaven. Therefore, when you do a charitable deed, do not sound a trumpet before you as the hypocrites do in the synagogues and in the streets, that **they may have glory from men**. Assuredly, I say to you, **they have their reward**. But when you do a charitable deed, do not let your left hand know what your right hand is doing, that your charitable deed **may be in secret**; and your Father **who sees in secret will Himself reward you openly**.*

—Matthew 6:1-4

*Moreover, when you fast, do not be like the hypocrites with a sad countenance. For they disfigure their face that they may appear to men to be fasting. Assuredly, I say to you, **they have their reward**. But you, when you fast, anoint your head and wash your face, so that you do not appear to men to be fasting, but to your Father who is in the secret place; and your Father **who sees in secret will reward you openly**.*

—Matthew 6:16-18

*For **nothing** is secret that will not be revealed, nor **anything hidden** that will not be known and come to light.*

—Luke 8:17

FAITH COMES BY HEARING

When Jesus was here, He did so many miracles that John said the books of the world couldn't contain them all (John 21:25). So then, the stories that we find recorded in the four gospels are hand-picked by the Holy Spirit, because He inspired Matthew, Mark, Luke, and John to write what they wrote. As children of God entrusted with the gospel, let's look at some of them and see how they pertain to the importance of accountability and availability.

> **When she heard about Jesus,** she came behind Him in the crowd and touched His garment. For she said, "if only I may touch His clothes, I shall be made well." Immediately the fountain of her blood was dried up, and she felt in her body that she was healed of the affliction.
>
> —Mark 5:27-29

Out of hundreds if not thousands of miracle testimonies those 4 men could've written down for us, the Spirit of God included the story about the woman with the issue of blood. I think His reasoning for this is obvious. We can be instrumental in someone else's miracle just by taking the time to tell others about what Jesus did for us, or for others. There's nothing grand or glorious about it. Just do what you can, and God will do what you can't. Someday when it counts up in heaven, everyone will know what was done to share Jesus with others. In this story, who is the person who told this sick woman about what Jesus was doing? It says that when she *heard about Jesus*, she started on the journey that led to that miraculous healing. Somebody had to tell her, but we'll never know who in this life—but we will in the next! God saw the exchange between the sick woman and the unknown somebody who told her about the miracle ministry of Jesus. That unknown somebody brought hope to a woman who had lost all hope. Imagine! *Twelve years* of bleeding. All her money spent trying to secure a cure. All avenues of medical assistance gone. But what she heard started a process that turned her hopeless situation around.

THE UNKNOWN SOMEBODY

And He looked around to see her who had done this thing. But the woman, fearing and trembling, knowing what had happened to her, came and fell down before Him and told Him the whole truth. And He said to her, **"Daughter, your faith has made you well.** *Go in peace, and be healed of your affliction."*

—Mark 5:32-34

How did this woman use her faith for healing? *She said something because she heard something.* This is always the way it works concerning the things we need from God. We hear or read something from God, and believe it in our heart. We then speak the desired end-result with our mouth (Romans 10:8-10), and what we say comes to pass (Mark 11:22-24). The doing is God's part, but the receiving can't happen until somebody speaks forth truth from the Word of God. That's our part.

And all across the world, how many times each day are believers busy about the Father's business in this way? It's possible the person or people who told this woman about Jesus never knew how their involvement was a significant and necessary piece in the puzzle that culminated in her miracle. Not only that, it's possible they never knew the long-term effects of her miracle, as she went around preaching the gospel because of her own experience and testimony. We'll get more into this when we reach the chapter that talks about the length of the line behind us on judgment day. In short, we don't have to be the person out front, shining in the spotlight. We just need to be the piece of the puzzle that completes the picture that God is assembling for those He sends us to. Little pieces. Going the extra mile. Random acts of kindness and generosity. Being available to help with no thought of repayment from those in need. Sharing a gospel verse, or a kind word of encouragement, or counsel to those in need. There are limitless ways we can work in the shadows like this, being an unknown somebody that God can count on to "get the ball rolling" in someone's life.

SEIZING THE OPPORTUNITY

> And **let us not grow weary** while doing good, for in due season we shall reap if we do not lose heart. Therefore, **as we have opportunity**, let us do good to all, especially to those who are of the household of faith.
> —Galatians 6:9-10

If believers understood the awesome honor and responsibility of being entrusted with the gospel, they'd be much better at seizing opportunities to share the truth with those in need. An incident recorded in the gospels illustrates the point:

> And being in Bethany at the house of Simon the leper, as He sat at the table, a woman came having an alabaster flask of very costly oil of spikenard. Then she broke the flask and poured it on His head. But there were some who were indignant among themselves, and said, "Why was this fragrant oil wasted? For it might have been sold for more than three hundred denarii and given to the poor." And they criticized her sharply. But Jesus said, "Let her alone. Why do you trouble her? She has done a good work for Me. For you have the poor with you always, and whenever you wish you may do them good, but Me you do not have always. **She has done what she could.** She has come beforehand to anoint My body for burial. Assuredly, I say to you, wherever this gospel is preached in the whole world, **what this woman has done will also be told as a memorial to her.**"
> —Mark 14:3-9

THE UNKNOWN SOMEBODY

I've said it many times, and I'll say it again. God never asks us to do what we can't. But He expects us to do what we can. *When we do what we can, God does what we can't.* Here we see what an unknown somebody can do when they just obey God and share some good, gospel news with people. While Jesus dined with Simon the leper and His disciples, it says *a woman came.* Why did she come? Because obviously, someone told her that the Lord was there. If someone hadn't told her, she wouldn't have been able to see and seize that opportunity to do a good deed for Jesus. And as "icing on the cake," Jesus told His complaining disciples that not only had she been a blessing to Him that day, but what she had just done would be told and retold tens of thousands of times afterwards—and you and I are doing exactly that today. We're reading about what an unknown somebody did because they were entrusted with sharing the good news with others—and took advantage of the opportunity. Just like we're entrusted to do the same today.

So, someday in heaven, when the rewards ceremony is being conducted, we'll get to meet the two unknown people that God used to bless His Son Jesus that day at Simon's house. We'll get to meet and know the woman who poured the expensive perfume on Jesus to bless Him, but we'll also get to meet the unknown somebody who told her where He was. And like with all of these stories we read about, *everyone involved* with an act of obedience like this gets the same reward in heaven.

This wasn't the only time somebody who was a nobody did this to Jesus. In Luke 7:37-50, the Holy Spirit provides us with another detailed example of what can be done when we seize the opportunity in the name of Jesus. In that story, it was a local prostitute, recently convicted of her sinful lifestyle, who came with a repentant heart and did what she could with another alabaster flask of costly perfume. None of this bothered Jesus. However, everybody else at the Pharisee's house was shocked and repulsed by this scene, where this "sordid" woman was ministering to

Jesus in the only way she could, trying to express to Him her heartfelt pleas for forgiveness and repentance. In the end, Jesus told her it was *her faith* that saved her. The Bible says that *when she knew that Jesus sat at the Pharisee's table*, she came to present herself to Him. So once again, I ask the question. Who told her that Jesus was in town, dining at the Pharisee's house? Somebody did—an unknown somebody. Unknown to us, but well known to God. The Bible is full of stories like this, if we have eyes to see them.

DOES THE LORD NEED WHAT YOU HAVE?

> *Now when they drew near Jerusalem, and came to Bethphage, at the Mount of Olives, then Jesus sent two disciples, saying to them, "Go into the village opposite you, and immediately you will find a donkey tied, and a colt with her. Loose them and bring them to Me. And if anyone says anything to you, you shall say, 'The Lord has need of them,' and **immediately he will send them**. All of this was done that it might be fulfilled which was spoken by the prophet, saying: "Tell the daughter of Zion, 'Behold, your King is coming to you, lowly, and sitting on a donkey, a colt the foal of a donkey.'"*
>
> —Matthew 21:1-5

Who owned the donkey and the colt? We don't know, but God does. When the two disciples went to say and do as instructed, the owners wanted to know what they were doing, exactly as Jesus predicted (see also Mark 11:1-7 and Luke 19:28-34). Answering the way Jesus told them to, the owners allowed two total strangers to walk off with their donkey and colt, simply because they were told that the Lord needed them. All of this was being done in fulfillment of prophecies regarding Jesus, their Messiah. Since there isn't any record the two disciples stopped to have an impromptu Bible study with the owners, it's fair to say they didn't know what was happening. They couldn't see the "bigger picture."

Here they were, taking part in a major Messianic prophecy being fulfilled right in front of them, and they were clueless as to the significance of their decision to let these two strangers take away their donkey and colt, with no apparent promise of bringing them back. And that's the point we need to see. When God is at work in people's lives, many times He calls upon us to get involved with our time, talents, and resources. We may never know to what extent our obedience played a part in someone being saved, healed, or recovered from the snares of the devil, but God knows—and will reward us accordingly in heaven. All God needs is our obedience, and total availability, with who we are and with what we have.

BE OBEDIENT AND ON TIME

> Now an angel of the Lord spoke to Philip, saying, "Arise and go toward the south along the road which goes down from Jerusalem to Gaza." This is desert. **So he arose and went.** And behold, a man of Ethiopia, a eunuch of great authority under Candace the queen of the Ethiopians, who had charge of all her treasury, and had come to Jerusalem to worship, was returning. And sitting in his chariot, he was reading Isaiah the prophet. Then the Spirit said to Philip, "Go near and overtake this chariot." So Philip **ran to him, and heard him reading the prophet Isaiah**, and said, "Do you understand what you are reading?"
>
> —Acts 8:26-30

Let's stop here for a moment, and consider what has happened. Philip the evangelist (Acts 21:8) had an angel from heaven unexpectedly appear with divine instructions. He was told to get up and head south along the road from Jerusalem to Gaza, which was out in the desert. Its noteworthy that his assignment required him to go into the *desert*. Traveling through the desert is not a fun-filled excursion of comfort and ease. It's a very harsh, unforgiving environment. It wasn't like he was being told to head over to the 5-star casino hotel, stay in one of their penthouse suites and be a keynote speaker for another "prosperity seminar." He was told to go out into a very hard and difficult place alone—and he wasn't told anything else. That represents the fact that when God calls us into action, we're to snap to attention, salute, and go wherever we're told to go, no matter who is or isn't coming with us, or how foreboding the location may be.

So, without knowing who or why he is being told to immediately drop everything and go south into the desert, the Bible says *he arose and went*. That means he was obedient to the leading of the Lord, no questions asked. He doesn't know there's a very important and influential eunuch sitting in a chariot in the middle of the desert, reading from the scroll of the prophet Isaiah. He doesn't know this man has great authority under Candace the Queen of Ethiopia. He also doesn't know he happens to be in charge of all of the Queen's treasury—wealth that God wants to tap into for funding the gospel nationwide. He doesn't know that because in all of this, he's a very important part of God's plan to introduce the life-saving gospel to the entire country of Ethiopia.

He doesn't know any of this because God didn't choose to tell him. *He just wants Philip to trust and obey.* So when he saw this man sitting in his chariot and reading one of the Old Testament scrolls, he heard the Holy Spirit tell him to run quickly and overtake the man. Why? Because God wants him to be within earshot as the eunuch gets to what we now know to be Chapter 53 of Isaiah, where he just happens to be reading the prophetic scriptures describing and identifying the Messiah. As Philip gets up to the chariot, he asks the eunuch if he understands what he is reading. He replies and says no, and here's what happened next:

> And he said, "How can I, unless someone guides me?" And he asked Philip to come up and sit with him. The **place in the Scripture which he read** was this: "He was led as a sheep to the slaughter; and as a lamb before its shearer is silent, so He opened not His mouth. In His humiliation His justice was taken away, and who will declare His generation? For his life is taken from the earth." So the eunuch answered Philip and said, "I ask you, of whom does the prophet say this, of himself or of some other man?" Then Philip opened his mouth, and **beginning at this Scripture, preached Jesus to him**.
>
> —Acts 8:31-35

Continue reading to the end of Acts Chapter 8. Once Philip accurately presented the gospel, the eunuch immediately received Jesus as Lord and Savior. He was then baptized in water, and continued on home to spread the good news far and wide, using his high government position to do so. Two men were used by God to introduce the gospel to the nation of Ethiopia. One man was identified, but the other one wasn't. Philip's key role in this encounter is obvious, but the unnamed eunuch is just as important because without his evangelism once he returned home, untold multitudes of people might never have heard the saving gospel. We'll find out who the eunuch is when we meet him on rewards day in heaven. But both men, known and unknown, will be rewarded in heaven for what was accomplished that day on the desert road, and for years afterwards throughout the country of Ethiopia.

NAME RECOGNITION ISN'T NECESSARY

> *And it happened, while Apollos was at Corinth, that Paul, having passed through the upper regions, came to Ephesus. And **finding some disciples** he said to them, "Did you receive the Holy Spirit when you believed?" So they said to him, "We have not so much as heard whether there is a Holy Spirit." And he said to them, "Into what then were you baptized?" So they said, "Into John's baptism.*
>
> —Acts 19:1-3

In this story, Paul's travels take him to the city of Ephesus. There he discovers a group of about twelve men that he thinks are born again, but finds out they're actually unsaved disciples of John the Baptist. He proceeds to preach Jesus to them. He leads them into the born again experience, followed by the laying on of hands to receive the baptism of the Holy Spirit. These new Christian believers start speaking with tongues and prophesying. This incurs the wrath of local Jewish believers, who reject the gospel and force Paul to take his newly born again and Holy Spirit baptized disciples to a "neutral" site—the school of Tyrannus (Acts 19:4-9). Now notice the next verse:

> *And this continued for two years, so that **all who dwelt in Asia heard the word of the Lord Jesus**, both Jews and Greeks.*
>
> —Acts 19:10

Paul found "some unknown, unnamed disciples," and that's all God needed to create an evangelistic juggernaut that covered the entire peninsula of Asia Minor in just two years, without the benefit of all the modern tools and technology we have today at our disposal. We don't know who they were, and we don't need to know. The Holy Spirit didn't think it was necessary for us to know them by name, because earthly recognition doesn't matter. God sees in secret, and will openly reward every faithful, fruitful worker in heaven someday soon, where it really counts.

From then until now, millions of saints worldwide have done exactly what these few disciples did, without any fanfare or public accolades. They didn't care if they were recognized or noticed by men, because it wasn't important to them. Once they got saved, they just went out there and did the work of the Lord. And from those small beginnings, God used their enthusiasm to win many more to Jesus in a very short window of time! The numbers of saved people could be in the thousands, tens of thousands or more—only God knows. This is how outreach results go from addition (Acts 2:41,47, 5:14, 11:24) to multiplication (Acts 9:31, 12:24). That group of around twelve men were called "some disciples," and what a group they were! They were just unknown somebodies, partnering anonymously with the Holy Spirit to win multitudes to Jesus.

THOSE WHO THROW NEED THOSE WHO DON'T

We all know the story of David and Goliath. It's told and retold time and again, all over the world. And indeed, someday we'll be there to witness the eternal rewards given to David for what he did in throwing the stone, killing the giant, and saving the nation of Israel. But on that wonderful day, before Jesus gives the rewards to David, He's going to call forth two unknown individuals who were instrumental in the great victory wrought on the day David killed Goliath. Let's find out who they were.

> *Then Jesse said to **his son David**, "Take now for your brothers an ephah of this dried grain and these ten loaves, and run to*

your brothers at the camp. And carry these ten cheeses to the captain of their thousand, and see how your brothers fare, and bring back news of them."

—1 Samuel 17:17-18

Now, in reading the entire chapter of 1 Samuel 17, we know that Jesse and his youngest son David knew there was an impending battle between the Jews and the Philistines. Jesse's three oldest sons were amongst the soldiers serving in the army under King Saul. David had visited the front lines on more than one occasion, to check up on things and report back to his father and continue tending his father's sheep. What they didn't know is that since David's last visit, Goliath had presented himself in the valley between the two armies—with taunting insults and challenges twice a day for forty days. So, just like before, here comes David with bread and cheese for his brothers.

While they're together and talking, here comes Goliath for challenge number 81. Although the rest of the army had heard the previous 80 challenges, this is the first time David heard them. The kid goes ballistic, incredulously asking why nobody has gone down there to kill the heathen and remove this reproach to God and His people. When everybody points out the size of this man (who also had an armor bearer in front of him), David famously declares victory because of the covenant they have with God. We know what happened next. He went down into the valley and killed the giant. This then inspired the entire army to rally to the cause, and slaughter all the retreating Philistine soldiers. But for David to do what he did, there were two other unknown somebodies who had to do their jobs first.

*So David rose early in the morning, **left the sheep with a keeper**, and took the things and went as Jesse had* *commanded him. And he came to the camp as the army was going out to the fight and shouting for the battle. For Israel and the Philistines had drawn up in battle array, army against army. And David* **left his supplies in the hand of the supply keeper**, *ran to the army, and came and greeted his brothers. Then as he talked with them, there was the champion, the Philistine of Gath, Goliath by name, coming up from the armies of the Philistines; and he spoke according to the same words.* **So David heard them.**

—1 Samuel 17:20-23

When David heard the giant's challenge, he did what he did to save the nation. He threw the stone, and he'll be rewarded for doing that. But how about the sheep keeper and the supply keeper? Nothing exciting about what their part in this great victory was, but nonetheless critical to the outcome as recorded in Scripture. Sitting under a tree somewhere watching sheep. Sitting back in the supply tent, staring at the supplies needed for the army to function. Boring, boring, boring. Little did they know the significance of their work—as mundane as it may have seemed to them. We don't know their names, but we will someday in heaven, when Jesus asks them to come up and stand with David for the rewards earned for saving the nation that day. Jesus will look at David and say: "Well done, good and faithful servant! You confronted the giant, threw the stone and killed him."

Then, He will turn to David's left and say to the sheep keeper and say: "Well done, good and faithful servant! You kept the sheep, and that enabled David to leave and come to the front lines to hear the giant's challenge. If you hadn't done that, David here wouldn't have been in position to do what he did." Then, He will turn to David's right and say to the supply keeper: "Well done, good and faithful servant! You kept David's supplies, and that enabled David to leave and come up the front lines to hear the giant's challenge. If you hadn't done that, David here wouldn't have been in position to do what he did." The Lord will then bestow equal recognition and rewards to the three of them.

Listen! For every stone thrower whom we know, there are untold multitudes of unknown sheep keepers and supply keepers. Unknown to us, but never unknown to God! The stone thrower *always* needs the keeper of the sheep and supplies, and vice versa! Everyone connected to an outreach assignment is just as important as everyone else in the mix. The unknown somebody is entrusted to complete their particular assignment behind the scenes, just as much as those who are publicly out in front. It takes everybody doing their part—everybody being entrusted to understand the importance of faithfulness to God, with or without public knowledge and acknowledgement.

EVERYBODY NEEDS EVERYBODY ELSE

> *If the foot should say, "Because I am not a hand, I am not of the body," is it therefore not of the body? And if the ear should say, "Because I am not an eye, I am not of the body," is it therefore not of the body? If the whole body were an eye, where would be the hearing? If the whole were hearing, where would be the smelling? But now* **God has set the members, each one of them, in the body just as He pleased.** *And if they were all one member, where would the body be? But now indeed there are many members, yet one body. And the eye cannot say to the hand, "I have no need of you," nor again the head to the feet, "I have no need of you."*
>
> —1 Corinthians 12:15-21

THE UNKNOWN SOMEBODY

Romans 12:16 explicitly tells us not to be wise in our own eyes. Romans 15:5 tells us to be like-minded towards each other. First Peter 3:8 exhorts us all to be of one mind. Philippians 2:2 says we're to be like-minded with the same love, being of one accord and of one mind. So then, the moment we start thinking we're somebody special, we're in trouble before the Lord! This extensive passage in 1 Corinthians is put there expressly by the Holy Spirit to remind us of these things. Although we see that there are five "ministry" gifts in Ephesians 4:11-12, those gifts are only as effective as the unknown somebodies who support them. Let's continue to see this from 1 Corinthains Chapter 12.

> *No, much rather those members of the body **which seem to be weaker are necessary**. And those members of the body which **we think** to be less honorable, on these we bestow greater honor; and our **unpresentable parts** have greater modesty, but our presentable parts have no need. But God composed the body, having given **greater honor to that part which lacks it**, that there should be no schism in the body, but that the members should have the same care for one another. And if one member suffers, all the members suffer with it; or if one member is honored, all the members rejoice with it.*
>
> —1 Corinthians 12:22-26

Notice carefully some of the key points here. Members of the body which *seem to be weaker are necessary*, and members of the body *which we think to be less honorable* should receive greater honor. That means God will actually give greater honor to those who didn't initially have it. In other words, the unknown somebody will not only be given great honor and rewards in heaven someday, but may actually get *more* than those we knew and were aware of. Think about that for a moment!

Entrusted for Eternity

The unknown brethren working in the shadows might seem to some of us to be weaker and less important, but the exact opposite is true from God's viewpoint! Praise God for these things! No matter what part you play as entrusted gospel bearers, your part is *very important*, and *very necessary*. Don't ever let the devil or those he uses convince you otherwise.

> *Knowing, therefore, the terror of the Lord, we persuade men;* ***but we are well known to God****, and I also trust are well known in our consciences.*
>
> —2 Corinthians 5:11

What we know or don't know about what fellow believers are doing doesn't matter. Our judgment of a person's worth to the cause isn't important either. It's enough to know that not everybody has the same number of "talents" (Matthew 25:14-29). We don't know everything about every situation we're called by God to be involved with. Our knowledge of who is doing what for Jesus is *always* extremely limited at best. That's why Romans 14:4 says what it says: *Who are we to judge another man's servant?* Other believers don't answer to us, and we don't answer to them. We all answer to God, and that should be an extremely comforting truth, since we know He sees everything.

> *"Can anyone hide himself in secret places,* ***so I shall not see him?****" says the Lord; "do I not fill heaven and earth?" says the Lord.*
>
> —Jeremiah 23:24

Everything said or done in secret will be openly revealed and proclaimed at each person's day of judgment. Believers will be rewarded accordingly, and sinners will be punished accordingly. Of this you can be sure.

THE UNKNOWN SOMEBODY

AN UNKNOWN SOMEBODY IS NEVER UNKNOWN TO GOD

I will take time in this book to share some of the details of my early beginnings as a soldier in the army of the Lord, because I want you to see how important the unknown somebodies were in helping me find my lane and run my race for Jesus. I know who they are, but after that, very few know how important they were in getting me to the place where God could use me as He has. God knows who they are, and how important they were in His plan for my life. Sometimes they understood the importance of doing their part, and sometimes they didn't. That's why we do what we do for the Lord, knowing it will always pay off in this life, and more importantly, in the next.

> And **whatever you do in word or deed**, do all in the name of the Lord Jesus, giving thanks to God the Father through Him.
> —Colossians 3:17

> And **whatever you do, do it heartily, as to the Lord and not to men**, knowing that from the Lord you will receive **the reward of the inheritance**; for you serve the Lord Christ.
> —Colossians 3:23-34

THE BOOK OF REMEMBRANCE

Each believer is critically important to God in the business of evangelism and discipleship. Every one of us. We don't have to know every little detail about what our work for God produced in this life. We only need to remember that we've been entrusted with the gospel. That means we are *accountable*, and so we must always be *available*.

> *Those who feared the Lord spoke to one another, and the Lord listened and heard them;* **so a book of remembrance was written** *before Him for those who fear the Lord and who meditate on His name.*
>
> —Malachi 3:16

Notice that this book of remembrance is not written for everybody. It's only written for those who fear the Lord, and meditate on His name. Once again, the scriptures emphasize the wonderful truth that everything a believer does for Jesus in this life is noticed, recorded, and will someday be rewarded.

In my life in Christ, all of these unknown nobodies to men are unknown somebodies to God. And there are many others I could make mention of as well. I wouldn't be who God's grace has made me today if it wasn't for Christians like these. They weren't polished preachers or anointed teachers of the gospel. They were just available and accountable to God, and took advantage of the opportunities afforded to them by the Holy Spirit.

> *And let us not grow weary while doing good, for in due season we shall reap if we do not lose heart. Therefore,* **as we have opportunity***, let us do good to all, especially to those who are of the household of faith.*
>
> —Galatians 6:9-10

> *For in this the saying is true:* **'One sows and another reaps.'** *I sent you to reap that for which you have not labored; others have labored, and you have entered into their labors.*
>
> —John 4:37-38

THE UNKNOWN SOMEBODY

Who then is Paul, and who is Apollos, but ministers through whom you believed, as the Lord gave to each one? I planted, Apollos watered, but God gave the increase. So then neither he who plants is anything nor he who waters, but God who gives the increase. Now he who plants and he who waters are one, and **each one will receive his own reward according to his own labor***.*

—1 Corinthians 3:5-8

EVERYBODY HAS AN UNKNOWN SOMEBODY TO THANK

Who are the people responsible for leading you to the Lord Jesus? I don't know who they are, but you do. To me, they are an unknown somebody, but to you they are a precious gift from God. And whatever you've done for Jesus since the day you got saved, those same people will stand with you to receive whatever rewards are handed out to you in heaven. That truth should encourage all of us.

CHAPTER 19

THE LENGTH OF THE LINE

*The refining pot is for silver and the furnace for gold. And a man is **valued by what others say of him**.*

—Proverbs 27:21

Everybody who loves Jesus and feeds upon the Word of God can point to certain passages that became a significant piece of the rock that their lives were built upon (Matthew 7:24-26). The foundation and cornerstone in my life as a believer includes this verse here in Proverbs. For a long time I would read that statement and ponder its meaning. One day in prayer the Lord gave me the explanation—one which blessed me then, and has blessed me ever since. I frequently think about it.

In John 3:16, we have what many call "the most precious verse." *"For God so loved the world that He gave His only begotten Son, that whoever believes in Him should not perish but have everlasting life."* Jesus has told us that God loves everybody. He is no respecter of persons (Acts 10:34). As far as He is concerned, all people are cherished and loved with a love that's so deep, its beyond our ability to comprehend it (Ephesians

3:19). When it comes to God's love for us, that's something He chose to do apart from us. There is nothing a person can do to make God stop loving him or her. He is the One who determines who He loves, and has declared that *everybody* is loved equally in His eyes. But Proverbs 27:21 isn't talking about love. Its talking about *value*. From Vocabulary.com, here's a dictionary definition for the word "value," as a noun: *The quality (positive or negative) that renders something desirable or valuable.*

THE DIFFERENCE BETWEEN LOVE AND VALUE

God determines His love for us, but we determine our value to Him. How so, you might ask? Well, I asked the Lord that same question. Notice that this verse talks about what others say about us—not what God says about us. For an explanation of that verse and that truth, here's what He told me. On the day that each Christian stands before His judgment seat, as recorded in Romans 14:10 and 2 Corinthians 5:10, the length of the line of believers standing behind the Christian being judged determines their value to God while they lived on earth. The people in that line are all those a Christian, in the course of their lifetime, worked in the name of Jesus to lead them through the born again experience, or to help them with their walk with the Lord once saved.

Jesus said the longer the line, the more valuable that Christian was to God in their lifetime. The shorter the line, the less valuable they were to Him in the business of winning and discipling souls. And if there's no line behind the Christian standing there to be judged, their life was of no value to the Lord. Are these people saved? Yes, of course they are, but they didn't do anything meaningful for the Lord while they lived on earth, so they never developed any value to God's Word, which tells us to "occupy" until Jesus returns (Luke 19:13 KJV). That means they'll be eternally saved as children of God, but won't get any rewards in heaven.

In short, the more people we influence in a positive way regarding the things of God, the more valuable we become to God. Every time we share Jesus with people, our heavenly value increases. Every time we obey God and do what He asks us to do, our heavenly value increases. Every time we assist God in the business of salvations, healings, or victorious living, our heavenly value increases. The good news is that our value to God is completely up to us—because God has given us free will. We can choose to obey God—and be blessed and rewarded forever accordingly—or we can choose to disobey and live our selfish lives that are preoccupied with secular wants and desires. And don't make the mistake of comparing your life's work with anyone else's. Jesus put it this way in Luke 12:48: *to whom much is given, much is required*. In contrast, God's love for everyone remains constant all the days of our lives, no matter who we are. Jesus said God so loved *the world* that He gave His only begotten Son (John 3:16). Each human being is part of the world. He chooses to love everyone, and has no favorites. But our value to God is not up to Him—it's up to us. Let me give you a few examples from my ministry in the Philippines.

HIDDEN BEHIND THE COCONUT TREE

I had just started my missionary work in the Philippines in the early 80s, and I was holding an open-air crusade in a small farming village near the city of San Carlos, on the island of Negros. With my interpreter, we presented the gospel to a group of local villagers that numbered around 50 or so. We preached, I gave the altar call, and almost every hand in the crowd went up to indicate their desire to receive Jesus as Lord and Savior. They got saved, and after the laying on of hands (Mark 16:18), many of them were healed as well. We introduced the follow-up pastor to the crowd and gave him the names of those who attended the crusade. Afterwards, we closed down the meeting and moved on, which is what I've done over and over, in thousands of cities, towns and villages throughout the Philippine Islands.

Decades later, my National Director of Churches and I were talking about his ministry activities while I was back in the States for a season of church visitations. He told me that while attending a recent minister's conference in a city located in the southern parts of the island of Mindanao, he was talking to a fellow attendee who was an ordained pastor with the Foursquare Gospel denomination. As they were talking, the Foursquare Gospel pastor asked my pastor who he worked for, or who he was "under," as we say. When he mentioned my name, the Foursquare Pastor was surprised, and asked if this was the same "Mike Keyes" who was the missionary from America.

When my pastor verified that I was indeed the man he was working under, this Foursquare Pastor proceeded to explain that many years before, when I conducted that small crusade on the island of Negros, he was there. He said that at the time, he was unsaved and on his way to hell. Not only that, but on that particular afternoon he was drunk, hiding behind a coconut tree, listening to my preaching. When I gave the altar call to the people that day, and asked them to raise their hands to heaven, little did I know this man was doing the same thing, confessing Jesus as Lord and Savior right along with everyone else that afternoon. He said after receiving salvation behind the coconut tree, he was immediately made sober by the power of God, and eventually went on to enroll in a Bible school and became a full-time pastor with the Foursquare Gospel denomination.

God has a way of making things known to us when its necessary. If we find ourselves discouraged or depressed because life has taken its toll on us, we need to remember stories like this. It's been a consistent source of encouragement to me when I think of this Foursquare pastor. I will look for him on my judgment day because I know he'll be in the line behind me, *along with all the souls he ministered to as a Christian and as a pastor.* That's the beauty of this! We have no idea how far-reaching our acts of obedience become after we do what God tells us to do. When God asks for things you possess, or asks for your obedience to say or do what needs to be presented to people, *just obey and trust God!* I've said it before, and I'll continue to repeat myself. There will be many surprises in heaven on the day when rewards are passed out.

OUR GATE GUARDS

In the Philippines, our base of operations is a compound located in Ozamiz City, on the northwestern coast of Mindanao. Mindanao is the island where most of the Muslims live, along with any terrorist groups operating throughout the country. Foreigners like me and my family are prime targets for kidnapping, because that's how many of these groups get their money to continue harassing the government. That being said, our compound has two large iron gates, and 12' foot walls with barbed wire and broken glass all along the top. In addition, we employ gate guards, opening and closing the gates to handle all foot and vehicular traffic in and out of the compound. These guards are just simple Filipino citizens. They're education is high school level at best. They're not called into full-time ministry, and they speak very little English. In other words, they're nobody special in any sense of the word. But they man the gates and represent the first line of protection and defense for everybody living in the compound. That makes them very important members of our ministry team, even though they're not called into ministry activity like me and my staff are. Every so often, when I'm addressing our staff in morning devotions or other services, I remind them of this. I want my people to understand that these guards may not be called by God to preach or interpret like them, but are just as important to the success of our ministry operations as anyone else. I want everyone connected to our ministry to work together, realizing that we all need each other if we're to function at design capacity for Jesus. Whatever rewards we get in heaven for doing God's work in the Philippines, those gate guards are going to get the same rewards because they did their job as unto the Lord. So when Jesus is judging us in heaven someday, they'll be standing in my line—and I'll be standing in theirs!

CHAPTER 20

MARILYN'S LINE

If you ask Christians to identify key players who were used by God to bring them into the born again experience, everyone will have those special individuals that will forever stand out in their mind. For me, God used a young woman named Barbara Westerfield, whom I met in Spanish class in college in 1970. Shortly after our relationship got serious, she moved in with me and we lived together for eight years. We went through the college years as boyfriend and girlfriend, and continued our relationship after graduation. I got jobs in Toledo, Ohio, and she got jobs in Bowling Green, Ohio, where we lived as university students, and continued living together afterwards. We had our ups and downs during that time as a couple, but never got married. (As you know, this is a very common lifestyle for those who don't know Jesus).

I was raised in a devout Roman Catholic family, so I would still attend Mass occasionally, but by this time I was a very secular person in lifestyle. Barbara was raised in a home where her parents were devoted atheists. They made fun of people who went to church, referring to them as weaklings who couldn't make it in the world without the crutch of religion. Despite this difference, I got along with her family nicely, taking care to avoid the obvious differences in social perception on the subject of Christianity. I initiated a breakup in 1977, but a few months later, seeing how lonely I was and how much I actually missed her, pleaded with her to come back to me. She had already found a boyfriend out in California, but for reasons she at the time didn't understand, she came back. We know now this was all being orchestrated by the Lord, but at the time we were both clueless.

By the time 1978 rolled around, things were just as dry as they had been before our breakup. Our relationship was on its last legs. There was no joy anymore in our relationship, and we hardly talked to each other. I would go to work in the morning while she was still asleep, and get home around 6:00 p.m. each night. To avoid as much contact as possible, she got a job at Domino's Pizza, reporting for work at 4:00 p.m. and working until closing, which was between midnight and 1:00 a.m. in those days. When she got home from work, I would already be asleep. She would be sleeping when I went to work, and when she went to work, I wasn't home yet. When she got home from work, I was already sleeping, so we never saw much of each other—by design. This was done on purpose. That's how bad things had become for us as a couple.

She was not a pizza delivery person for Domino's. Instead, she worked in the shop making the pizza pies the drivers would take out for delivery (for those of you old enough to remember the Domino's pizza delivery trucks). There was already a young girl named Marilyn, working there when she was hired, so the two of them worked side by side every night making pizza pies. Marilyn was an on-fire-for-God Christian, singing praise songs to the Lord while she did her work. This initially bothered Barbara, but she had no choice but to put up with her singing and praising, since there was nothing she could do about it. Over time they struck up a friendship, and Marilyn would talk about her life and the situation she had with her husband and small children. All of this took place back in the mid-1970s, when there were shortages of gasoline and as a result, long lines at the gas pumps. It was a very difficult and trying time for the U.S. economy. Inflation was sky-high, and unemployment was also off the charts. That's why she had gone to work, because her husband had lost his job and they had three small kids to feed and care for. Marilyn shared all of this with Barbara as they would stand shoulder to shoulder, spinning the dough to make those pizzas.

GOD CAN USE PIZZA MAKERS

Finally, as Barb related it to me later, she asked Marilyn how she could be so joyful and happy, singing Christian songs like she did, night after night. Her car was a wreck, held together with Christian bumper stickers. You know what I'm talking about. It's the beat-up clunker driving down the road with the big, blue "glory cloud" coming out the tailpipe! Her husband was just a blue-collar type of factory worker who had just been laid off. She had three small kids, all of them still in diapers. They lived in an old, rundown mobile home in the soybean and corn fields of northwest Ohio in the dead of winter. I know, because Marilyn had invited the two of us to come out to their home for a dinner at some point during their employment time at Domino's. I can still picture that old, dilapidated mobile home they lived in. It was listing over badly to one side, and they had it tied to the ground so the wind wouldn't blow it over. That's why Marilyn took this dead-end job, because even though it paid minimum wage, it was the only source of income at the time for her family.

So, knowing all of this now that they had become friendly co-workers, Barbara asked straight up one night: "I know what kind of life you and your family have right now, *so please tell me why you are so joyful!*" Marilyn replied with a big smile and said, *"It's just Jesus!"* Remember, Barbara's family was populated by people who were either declared atheists, or clearly agnostic at best. So she began to analyze this situation as it applied to her life with me. Her she was, living with a young advertising executive earning a very good salary, living in a big, rented house on main street in Bowling Green, Ohio. There were two cars in the driveway, and lots of food in the kitchen—yet she and I were miserable! On the other hand, there was this young lady, who wasn't even physically attractive by the world's standards, but came into work smiling, singing, and bubbling over with a kind of joy that belied her terrible living conditions. Barbara just kept watching and listening over the space of many months, as Marilyn continued to exhibit the joy of the Lord while working her minimum-wage job. I didn't know any of this was going on, because by this time, as I said, we hardly talked to each other.

Meanwhile, my advertising responsibilities took me to New York City to find talent we were going to hire for some TV commercials the company was doing. I said goodbye and flew away. When I got home from that business trip three days later, I immediately saw that something was different about her. Usually, she would find ways to avoid me when I came in from an out-of-town trip like this, but this time she met at the front door as I was walking up the stairs (we lived on the second floor of a large, old mansion that had been divided up for renting purposes). I never will forget it. She had this smile from ear to ear, and there was a peaceful look on her face that I hadn't seen since the early days of our relationship. You know, when you live with someone for years, like we had, you can easily read facial expressions, and I could see she was somehow different—in a good sort of way. I asked her: *What happened to you?* She replied: *"It's just Jesus!"* I shouted out incredulously, *"Jesus?!"* She then told me she had given her heart to the Lord, and was born again. I didn't know what to say. We went into the house, and she sat me down and told me the whole story of what happened.

She told me that while I was away, she had gone into the living room, crying in the dark around midnight. She was wondering if it was time for us to break up for good. Nothing was working, and she was as miserable as I was. Then in a moment of heavenly inspiration, she remembered Marilyn from Domino's, and cried out to God. (Remember, being from a *very* antagonistic family when it came to Christianity, she didn't know how to pray because she had never prayed a prayer in her life). Not knowing any better, she just blurted out the cry of her heart: *"Jesus, if you're real, I want what that girl has at work."* She didn't know it at the time, but what she was really asking for was the joy that only a Christian can enjoy. She told me the moment she prayed this simple prayer; it seemed like someone was standing behind the couch, pouring a warm bucket of honey on her. She said it started at the top of her head, and slowly made its way down her body, out her arms and legs to the bottom of her feet. And just like that, she was instantly born again! Nobody was there with her that night, but it wasn't necessary because Marilyn had done what needed to be done. Over and over, night after night at Domino's, she let a lost, confused sinner see the love and joy that comes from being a child of God.

CHAPTER 21

BARBARA'S LINE

Thanks to Marilyn, Barbara reached out and was born again. That's why when I returned from my business trip to New York, she met me at the door with the joy of the Lord all over her. It was like she had been stumbling around in the dark all her life, and in a moment of time, the light had turned on and she knew the truth that set her free (John 8:32-36). She was so full of joy and happiness; she could hardly wait to share the good news with me. Well, being the good non-practicing Catholic as I was, I defended myself! I told her that was all well and good for her, and I was happy for her, but I already had Jesus, even though I didn't have any idea about what it meant to be born again.

Caring for my soul, she began to witness to me, not so much with Bible verses, because she didn't know anything about the Bible as a new baby Christian. Her witnessing was done more with the way she had changed in terms of demeanor and lifestyle. She was singing songs about Jesus, humming and going about the house with the joy of the Lord all over her. But as so many religious people do, I brushed off her attempts to witness to me, claiming that as a Catholic, I was already saved and didn't need to entertain her pleadings that I needed to be born again.

GOD CAN USE FIELD GOAL KICKERS

God works in mysterious ways. We've all heard that, haven't we? Well, in my case He certainly did. To reach my girlfriend Barbara, He used Marilyn the pizza maker. Now, to get my attention, He used my love for Cleveland sports teams to open my eyes to the true condition of my soul (I was born and raised in Cleveland, Ohio). One Sunday afternoon, I was sitting in the living room, watching the Cleveland Browns play the Cincinnati Bengals. This is a cross-state rivalry that is as intense as any could be. The Browns were winning the game by two points, but the Bengals had moved the ball downfield and with only a few seconds left on the clock, were going to kick a 3-point field goal and win the game by one point.

Their field goal kicker was in a groove, having not missed a field goal attempt in many tries—and they had the ball just a few yards from the Browns' goal line. It was so close the guy could've used his finger to kick the ball through the uprights. Barbara came into the room at that moment. She had no interest in football like me, so she had been doing other things around the house while I was watching this football game. She sees the look on my face and hears me mumbling about how my beloved team is about to lose the game by a point—to Cincinnati no less. Without hesitation, she sits down next to me and gently takes my hand and says to me, *"Oh, I'll just pray, and I'll ask Jesus to make that man miss that field goal, just to let Mike know how much you love him!"*

I stared at her like she just got off the bus from the planet Mars, but before I could protest, she prayed that simple prayer. Meanwhile, the Bengals' field goal team had come out on the field and lined up for the field goal attempt that would win the game. They snapped the ball, and their kicker kicked the ball. It didn't go straight through the uprights, as everyone in the stadium was expecting. It missed. But it didn't barely miss, it missed by a mile! The moment the ball left his foot, it careened off to the left like a dying duck. The cameraman couldn't even track it, it went awry so far and so fast.

Of course, with the game being played in Cleveland, the crowd was going wild with joy! But the TV then pans a close-up to the kicker's face, and he has this dumbfounded look on his face, trying to figure out why his kick missed so badly as it did. Then, the TV pans to their coach, who has a similar look of disbelief on his face. And as I'm sitting there myself, I hear Barbara in the kitchen lifting her hands in praise saying: *"Thank you, Lord. Thank you, Lord!"* I mean, she didn't even sit with me to watch to see if the kicker missed his kick or not. After she had prayed that simple heartfelt prayer, she got up and left the room! And I thought to myself, *you know, there's something to this born again business!* For the first time, that got me thinking about my own life and my true condition with regards to being "right" with God. But still I was a tough Catholic cookie to crack. I wouldn't yet commit to anything "spiritual," even after God did what He did during that football game.

By this time, Barbara was regularly attending Bethel Assembly of God, in Perrysburg, Ohio. Not long after that incident with the field goal kicker, she attended a weeknight Bible study, held at the house of one of their church elders. There was a tongue and interpretation of tongues given at the end. The gist of that word from God was that Jesus was coming soon, to get ready for Him because His return was very close—even at the door. This scared Barbara, knowing that I wasn't right with God, even though I thought that I was. She came home in tears, shaking and trying her best to once again get through to me. But once again, I brushed her off.

Not knowing what else to do, she went to the local Christian bookstore in downtown Bowling Green, searching for anything that could help her help me. On a revolving book stand, she found a little green and white mini book entitled *The New Birth*, by Kenneth E. Hagin. She didn't know him at all—had never heard of him or his ministry. But the new birth was what she was trying to get over to me, so she bought the mini book and took it to me. As I'm sitting on the couch watching TV later that evening, she charges in and flips the book at me in tears, saying to me, "Here stupid, read this book!" Having said what she said, she walked out and left.

PERSISTENCE PAYS OFF

I picked up the little book, read the cover title, and promptly put it down on the coffee table. But, out of curiosity, I took it to work the next day. When I read it on my lunch hour, the contents so convicted and scared me, I told my secretary I had to leave for a meeting and wouldn't be back for a while (even though there was no meeting for me scheduled that afternoon). I left the building and went down to the river park along the banks of the Maumee River and read the mini book again. For the first time, finally, after months and months of Barbara trying to get through me, my spiritual eyes were opened, and I realized I was lost and on my way to hell.

Remembering what Barbara had told me about what the Lord had said in that Bible study recently, I was terrified that He might come back *today*, and I would end up in hell forever. So, I followed the instructions laid out in Brother Hagin's book—four simple steps to follow to become a born again Christian. When I did that, I was born again at about 1:30 p.m. on 21 September 1978. It was a warm afternoon with a partly cloudy sky. There was no one around because everybody had already gone back to work after their lunch hour. My new birth was truly by faith, because I didn't feel any different. So much so, that I repeated those four steps a second time. I still had no "feeling!" I kept waiting for that warm bucket of honey *feeling* to pour all over me like what happened to Barbara, but nothing happened. But I knew that God knew I was sincere in what I had just said and done, so I decided to believe I was saved—the very first time I was walking by faith and not by sight—and didn't even know it!

EVANGELISM STARTED FOR ME ON DAY ONE

I went back to work, finished up and went home. Later that evening, before I had the chance to tell Barbara what had happened, I decided to just go over to the nearby Catholic campus church. As a nominal, non-practicing Catholic, that was the church I would go to for the Sunday Mass whenever I felt like it (which wasn't very often). The church is still there, named Saint Thomas More University Parish, and is situated right next to the Bowling Green State University campus, the school we both attended and graduated from years earlier. There were no services going on that evening, but they always left the doors open in case people needed to come in and pray. I went in and sat on the back row, in the shadows because there was only one light on in the whole sanctuary, way up at the front where the altar was.

I felt good inside, knowing what I had said and done earlier that day at work. I sat there for quite a while, just thinking about what it meant to be "born again," and what this meant going forward in my life. While sitting there in the dark, a coed college student came in and sat in a pew up front under the light. She had used a different entrance than me, so she didn't know I was sitting in the back in the dark. I watched her for some time, and it was obvious something was troubling her greatly. No doubt, this was why she had come to church to pray. Without thinking, I got up and walked down the center aisle up to the front, where she was sitting. At first, she was startled as I came up to her, since she hadn't been aware that I was even in the building. I didn't ask for her name, and I didn't give her mine. I simply said to her something like this: *"I don't know what has you so troubled, but it's obvious you're praying about something very important. All I can tell you is that Jesus is the only answer to your problem."*

Having said that to her, I turned and walked out and went home. I was born again around 1:30 p.m. that same afternoon. This incident happened around 7:00 p.m. that same night. It took God all of six hours or so to get me started with evangelism. If you had told me 24 hours earlier, that I would be in church witnessing and encouraging somebody—anybody—to seek Jesus for the help they needed, I would've told you you're crazy. But that's how everything started. From there I got plugged into the same church that Barbara had been attending, and over the next twelve months, my street witnessing ministry took off. I was born again in September 1978. I enrolled in Rhema Bible Training College in September 1979. I left for the Philippines as a full-time missionary in September 1980.

Barb and I both went to Rhema as first year students. I left after one year of study, but she stayed on for a second year of study, which at that time was optional. When it became clear to us that God's plan for my life was foreign missions and hers was not, we knew it was the right time to end our boyfriend/girlfriend relationship. The difference was that this time, it was orchestrated by the Lord, which made all the difference. A short time later she met her husband, who was also a Rhema Bible School student, and they were married in the summer of 1980, just a few months before I left for the Philippines. I was able to attend their wedding, and was genuinely happy for her, because we both knew this was what God wanted for us both going forward.

God used a simple, God-fearing, Jesus-loving pizza girl to witness to my girlfriend, who witnessed to me and set me on the path I've been on ever since. He used an errant field goal attempt to slap me upside the head, so to speak. The Lord entrusted these two women with the saving knowledge of the gospel, and did what they could to change this man's life forever. I'm just one example amongst millions of others who can share similar testimonies. It's just amazing how God can use everyday people, and everyday circumstances to bring people to the point of decision for salvation. That should encourage each and every Christian out there, including you!

The Bible says in the tribulation that is coming very soon, saints will overcome the devil by the blood of the Lamb, and the word of their testimony (Revelation 12:10). And as wonderful as this part of my testimony is, God wasn't finished setting me up for the life I've lived in Him ever since. As we hear in those late-night commercials for products we don't want or have never heard of, *but wait, there's more!*

ENDUED WITH POWER

Less than three months after I was born again, I experienced an encounter along these lines that has stayed with me all my life. It was early December 1978. I had been born again in September 1978, but I was still working a secular job as an Advertising Executive for Owens Corning, the international corporation specializing in residential and commercial insulation products. Between September and December, the Lord began dealing with me about answering the call into full-time ministry. The longer this went on, the harder it was for me to go to work each day. What used to excite me about my work no longer did so. I was just "on fire" for Jesus in every which way possible. During my lunch hour, no longer would I go out for food and drinks with fellow office workers. I just wanted to stay in my office cubicle, and read the Bible for 60 minutes. I was witnessing to everybody on my floor about Jesus, and I'm sure they're hated to see me coming towards them down the hall!

Being a new babe in Christ, I didn't know much about the Word of God, and how to effectively share it when witnessing to strangers. However, there was no question about my zealousness. Barbara and I continued to work on our relationship, but once I got born again, I knew it was wrong for us to live together and be intimate as we had been before. No one told me it was wrong to live together outside of marriage, but I just knew in my heart it couldn't continue. It was the Holy Spirit doing His work to separate me to the calling He had in store for me, much like He did with the Apostle Paul (Romans 1:1).

I helped her find a small apartment not far from our house, and she moved in there. We continued to see each other, but my life had been radically changed. All I wanted to do now was talk about Jesus and the need for being born again. The day after I received my salvation on the park bench, Barbara attended that same Bible study, and told them all about what had happened to me. They then told her that we both needed to be filled with the Holy Spirit, with the evidence of speaking in other tongues. She came home and told me about this. She didn't know anything more about this gift or what it is designed to do for the Christian, but when she told me about it, I was immediately open to receiving it. If it meant I would be more "on fire" for Jesus, I was game!

I asked her to explain this gift they told her about. She said they told her it's a marvelous gift that equips believers with more power to witness and represent Jesus, and that all we have to do is ask Him to give it to us. I then asked what happens after we ask. She said we will get "tongues," which are words we don't understand but which come out of our spirit, words which God understands even though we don't. She said that's all they told her, so in pure faith the two of us did what they told us to do. We asked in faith, and we both got the gift! Just like what happened to me on the park bench a few days beforehand, no minister or Christian was present to "assist." All by ourselves, we got the infilling with the Holy Spirit, and began speaking in tongues. In pure faith and simplicity, we both sat on the edge of the bed, holding hands, and asked the Lord to fill us with the Holy Spirit.

I'm sure God had a good chuckle over us, looking at these two new babes in Christ, holding hands and asking for the baptism of the Holy

Spirit. But I think He was well-pleased, nonetheless. He honored our simple and sincere faith, and that night we both began speaking in tongues. Wow! Finally there were those incredible "feelings" I had been looking for! Truly, it was a glorious experience for us that night. By now, I was religiously attending services at that same church in Perrysburg, Ohio with her, and I couldn't stop telling people about Jesus. It's all I wanted to do. I didn't care about work anymore. I didn't care about football games anymore. I didn't care about anything else—I wanted to tell people everywhere that they needed to be born again.

Because I didn't know much that was in the Bible, I attended every church service I could. I also started following several well-known ministries on the radio, and with their newsletters and magazines. And I did what I could—I started going out on weekends for street witnessing with Reverend Ronal Charles, who was at that time in charge of outreach and evangelism at the Bethel Church. But that wasn't enough for me—I had to be doing more than what we could do together.

To help me with my street witnessing, I got hold of a tract publication catalog from a company called Good News Publishers, based out of Chicago, IL. I would peruse through their many pages showing differing gospel tract designs, and after I picked out several that I liked, I would order large quantities and have them sent directly to my home address. At the peak of my evangelistic endeavors, I was ordering and distributing upwards of 5,000 tracts monthly. This was done on my own time with my own money. The church didn't pay for any of this, nor did they officially sanction me to do what I was doing. But after I got those tracts in hand, I went and had a rubber stamp made with the pastor's name, church address and phone number, and hand-stamped my tracts before I would pass them out. I had stamped tracts laid out on tables, chairs, and furniture all over my apartment, waiting for the ink to dry. Then I would scoop them up and start passing them out.

Entrusted for Eternity

I had tracts in my shirt, pants, and suitcase pockets. I had them in my business briefcase. I had tracts in the glove compartment of my car. I passed them out everywhere I could. I passed them out walking to and from the parking garage I used for parking my car for work each day. I passed out tracts on weekends at the Toledo Express Airport. For the airport ministry, using a lined yellow pad, I made a master list of all arriving and departing flights, and made sure I was at the gate to pass out tracts to incoming passengers, then I would zip down to another gate to hand out tracts to passengers waiting to depart on some other flight. I would go into the restrooms at the airport, and put tracts on all the toilet seats and sink tops. I put tracts underneath all the public phones in the airport. I went out into the short and long term parking lots, and put tracts under the windshield wipers of all the parked cars. I'd make my rounds every hour or so, picking up tracts people had thrown on the ground, and putting them on other cars that had come in since my last go-around.

The church I started going to didn't know I was doing this. Each tract was stamped *Pastor Dan Wood. Bethel Assembly of God. Perrysburg, OH*, even though Pastor Wood didn't know I was doing this. The church outreach department didn't know I was doing this. But each Sunday, I would walk up to Pastor Wood and hand him a handwritten list of the names of souls I had won to Jesus on the streets of Toledo, OH, where Owens Corning's headquarters are located, and Bowling Green, OH, where I lived at the time. I was thinking they had follow-up organized to reach out to these souls, but I found out they didn't. But as I continued doing this, they began asking: who are you? Where did you come from? But as a result of what I was doing, they decided to make me their assistant outreach director, under Associate Pastor Ronal Charles. Together, Pastor Charles and I would go out on weekends to witness and pass out tracts all over town. And when he wasn't available, I'd be doing the street evangelism by myself. This is how things were for me in December 1978.

CHAPTER 22

MAC'S LINE

At the time of my born again experience, I was well on my way to a successful career in corporate management. I was only 26 years old, and I had a well-paying job that had prosperity written all over it. But once I received my salvation, I became totally disinterested in continuing in that job—or any other for that matter. All I wanted to do was read my Bible, attend church, and witness for Jesus everywhere. Not only did I spend my lunch hours reading my Bible, but I even cut out from my office, and sat on the top of the toilet seat in the men's restroom, reading my pocket Bible for hours.

Of course, looking back, that was not the right thing to do with regards to my employer and what I was being paid to do, but I had such a burning desire to learn more about God, Jesus, and the Word of God. I had been raised in a Roman Catholic family, and had gone to Catholic grade school and Catholic high school. I knew all about God, and at one point in high school, I had seriously considered becoming a Catholic priest. But once I got into college, it took the devil all of three months to totally warp my mind and drag me into drugs, drinking, and many other sinful acts and activities. And most importantly, I wasn't saved. I was just a good Catholic person, unsaved and on my way to hell. So when I got saved and Spirit-filled two days later, on 23 September 1978, my whole world was turned upside down—and I loved it!

In short, by the time December 1978 rolled around, I knew it was just a matter of time before I would resign my job and do whatever I needed to do to get into full-time outreach ministry. This was the background that was in play when God used another unknown somebody to give me the first set of instructions related to His calling in my life. Earlier that day, Barbara had followed me to the car dealership, where my car was scheduled for routine maintenance. The arrangement was that she would then drive me in to work, and at the end of the day, pick me up at 5:30 p.m. at a certain street corner near the high-rise office building I worked at, and then drive me back to the dealership to pick up my car.

Well, the temperatures in the morning going to work were unseasonably warm, and neither of us bothered to check the weather forecast on the news the night before. Turns out, there was a blizzard forecast to come through during the day, but we didn't know that. So, I went to work without a winter coat, hat, or boots. Barb dropped me off and went home. Sure enough, later that day the forecasted storm rolled into town. When I came out from work at around 5:00 p.m., I came out to a full scale winter storm. The temperature had dropped considerably. The wind was howling, and the snow was coming down sideways because of the wind. Visibility was practically nil. I made it to the prescribed street corner to await my ride, but because of the storm, Barbara was late. She was stuck in freeway traffic, creeping along because of the storm. This was back before the days of The Weather Channel, the Internet, and smartphones, so I couldn't call her to find out where she was, and she couldn't call me to let me know when she would get there.

So, I'm standing on this street corner, freezing. I've got my suit lapels pulled up around my neck, and I'm blowing into my cupped hands while stomping my feet to try and keep my hands and feet warm. 5:30 p.m. comes and goes, and there's no sign of my ride. I'm praying,

MAC'S LINE

and trying to hang on until Barbara gets there, and as I'm standing there on that corner, I hear a big thud. I turn and look down to see where the noise came from, and I see a stack of newspapers. I look up and there stands an old black man. He didn't have to say a word, but I could just tell by looking at him that he was very poor. He had an old jacket that had several tears in the sleeves, big enough to see the insulation and lining of the coat. His hat, shirt, and pants were also old and weather-beaten. He had on a pair of those old, black rubber boots with the 4 or 5 fastener clips that you used to close the boot around your leg. He had no gloves.

We acknowledged each other with a nod and stood together on that street corner, trying to brave the elements as best we could. We started talking to keep our lips from freezing. I introduced myself, and told him I worked in that very tall high-rise building a couple of blocks away. He introduced himself, and told me he was also at work, trying to sell evening newspapers to the car drivers that would be stopped when the light was red. His name was Mac. Time goes by, and still no ride. We're both freezing on this street corner, but whenever the light was green and no cars were stopped at the light, we'd duck into a corner cubby to get some relief from the wind. Mac told me he lived not far from where we were, in a rundown section of the inner city. I knew where it was. He said this job selling newspapers was his sole source of income for him and his wife. Whatever he earned selling newspapers, that's what he would take home to live on.

As he's talking with me, he turns to me and says, "You look cold! If you watch my papers for a few minutes, I'll walk up to the coffee shop and buy you a cup of coffee." At that point, he had sold one newspaper. The name of the newspaper was *The Toledo Blade*, and back then they sold for .25 each. So, he had .25 in his pocket, which in those days was enough to buy one cup of coffee. Before I could say anything, he just put the papers down and took off across the street into the storm. It was such a surreal sight; I'll never forget it. Because of the storm, the whole downtown was deserted. There were no cars on the streets, and no pedestrians. Just him and I. All the stores had closed early because of the storm, but the only one left open was this little coffee shop about half a block up from the street corner where we were. You could barely see it through the wind-driven snow, but there it was. That's where Mac went to buy me a cup of coffee.

Five minutes later, he comes back with the one cup of coffee. That's all the money he had, and he used it to buy coffee for me. He was just as cold as I was, but he was thinking of my needs over his own. I had a briefcase full of money, and I could've gone to that coffee shop and bought gallons of coffee, but I didn't see the opportunity like he did. When he brought the coffee up to hand to me, I wrapped my fingers around his, in order to take the cup away. When I did, I felt his hands and they were like ice. Cold wouldn't be the right word. They were like frozen popsicles. The moment I wrapped my hand around his, God spoke up in my heart. He said to me: "You see what this man is doing to help you? This is what you're going to be doing for Me for the rest of your life in ministry." Just like that, and just as quick as that, God laid out His plan for my life as a child of God, and full-time minister of the gospel. He used this kind gesture from Mac to inform me that from eternity past, I had been earmarked to be entrusted with the gospel.

Now, in all of our street corner conversation, I never told Mac I was a newly born again Christian of just a few months. He didn't know that God was already dealing with me to resign my job with Owens Corning, and go into some type of full-time ministry. Some of the details of my initial calling didn't come until almost a year later while I was a student at Rhema in Tulsa, Oklahoma, but this was the first time God had spoken to me about my future in Christ. Mac knew none of this was happening in my spirit as he handed me that .25 cup of coffee, *but I did, and God did.*

MAC'S LINE

A few minutes later, Barbara my driver showed up and took me to the dealership to get my car. I was surprised the dealership was still open because of the storm, but it was. When I got picked up and then afterwards, while driving my car home, I cried and cried. Mac's simple act of Christian kindness made such an impact on me—not to mention what God had specifically told me about what I would be doing for Him from now on. When I got home to Bowling Green, Ohio, where I still lived after graduating from BGSU in 1973, there was a Walmart-type store still open. I drove over there as fast as I could before they closed, and went to the aisle where they had winter gloves for sale. I just took a guess as to the proper size of Mac's hands, and bought a pair of the warmest gloves they had. I put those gloves in my briefcase, and for 2 weeks I hunted up and down the streets of downtown Toledo, looking for him. I remembered that he told me he moved around from street corner to street corner, so I had to just keep looking until I accidentally found him selling his newspapers.

One Friday morning, as I was walking into work a few weeks after the events of that stormy winter night, I saw him walking away from me, about a block and a half away. I recognized him immediately. He had on the same clothing he had worn the night we met, and he had his paper bag slug across his shoulder and back, which he used to carry his newspapers in. I ran up to him, very excited to see him again. At first, he didn't recognize me, but when I told him who I was, his face lit up and he remembered me. I told him how blessed I was with how he had bought me that cup of coffee a few weeks back during the blizzard, and I told him that I had noticed he didn't have any gloves on that night. Having said that, I reached down, opened my briefcase and pulled out the pair of winter gloves I had bought for him. I told him this was the least I could do to show appreciation for how he demonstrated such kindness with the cup of coffee he bought for me. As we stood there for a few minutes talking, he never put the gloves on. He just held them between his hands, stroking them back and forth, top to bottom. As he did this, he told me he had never had a nice pair of gloves like this, and was so very thankful. Well, I told him I needed to go, or I'd be late for work. We hugged and parted ways. I've never seen him since, and I've often wondered if he was a Christian. I thought he was, but I wasn't sure, until God orchestrated circumstances years later to let me know, in ways only He can.

Thirty five years later, I was sharing this story during a Sunday morning message, thousands of miles away in San Bernardino, CA. As I was handling product sales at our resource table in the lobby after service, a middle-aged black brother came up and told me he personally knew Mac! He told me that he grew up and lived in the same downtown Toledo neighborhood as Mac and his wife. He said everybody knew him in their community. I asked if he knew if Mac was a born again Christian, and he said that he was. Needless to say, I was so happy to hear this, and took time to thank and praise God for addressing my questions in this matter. He's done this with me a number of times over the years. Sometimes it takes years for answers or revelations to come, but the Lord has a way of letting us know what's important to our work for Him, doesn't He? With all that's going on in the world at any given moment, what are the chances of having a divinely arranged encounter with a Christian that God used to let me know what I wanted to know about another divinely orchestrated event that blessed me so much almost 40 years before? Incredible!

CHAPTER 23

NORVEL'S LINE

God was not finished preparing me for overseas missions work. During my time as a First Year Rhema student, Rev. Kenneth E. Hagin had Brother Norvel Hayes come to town and be his substitute teacher for a week during their prayer and healing classes they had started recently on campus. During my year there, I wasn't able to attend many of the special meetings with guests ministers because of my job as the Night Man at a local Quik Trip convenience store. I would go to work at 10:30 p.m., start my shift at 11:00 p.m., then work until 7:00 a.m., go home to get cleaned up for Rhema classes, which started at 8:30 a.m. This was my life for my whole time as a Rhema student. But God knew what I needed, and made sure I was able to attend one of Brother Norvel's evening classes on prayer and healing.

That night, he ministered extensively on Acts Chapter 9, about how the Lord met Saul on the road to Damascus, and how that encounter with God's power changed this man from Saul to Paul, and launched the ministry for one of the greatest New Testament apostles that we know of. At the end of his message, he called for all the people in the audience who knew they were called as missionaries to foreign countries. I was one of about 25 people who came up, and I was the last one in line to his left as he faced the congregation. He told everyone in the line that he would lay hands on each of us, and when he did, the same anointing that came upon the Apostle Paul that day on the road to Damascus would be imparted to us. He started laying hands on people to his right, which meant I would be the last one he'd lay hands on going from his right to his left.

The anointing on him and in the room was so thick people were having a hard time standing up, waiting for him to get to them in the line. I myself was teetering under the anointing myself, but managed to stay upright until he finally reached me. When he did, he barely brushed one finger across my forehead, and I went down to the floor like a sack of rocks. I lay on the floor for at least 45 minutes, with God's power surging through me like electricity. It was like someone had plugged me into an electrical socket, and was turning the power on then off, on then off. My lips were quivering, my eyes flickering, and I could barely hear what was going on around me, as Norvel ministered deliverance and healing to others after me.

On the floor, I cried out to the Lord, asking Him what this was, and He said to me, "Well, you've been standing in faith for miracle power overseas in the Philippines, and now you're getting it." It was incredible and unlike anything I've received before or after in my walk with God. Brother Norvel closed the service and dismissed everyone and left the building—and I was still on the floor, unable to get up. The janitor patiently waited for me, and after about 45 minutes, I managed to get up, walk out to my car and only by God's grace, drive home safely! I was drunk in the Spirit for hours afterwards. I did have the chance to meet Brother Norvel a couple of years later when he spoke at Rev. Buddy Harrison's church in Tulsa during one of my return visits to the States, and I told him what he had said and done that night. I'm happy to report he was very blessed by what I told him. In fact, I did go overseas with this anointing, and I've not only carried it ever since, but I've been instructed by God to impart that same anointing many times in church meetings and prayers lines around the world.

KEY PLAYERS IN MY LIFE

Marilyn doesn't know what chain of events were set in motion when she was singing her love songs to Jesus next to Barbara at Domino's Pizza. Barbara knows that I left the USA to start missions work in the Philippines, but she doesn't know the extent of what the Lord has used me to do overseas. When Mac bought me that cup of coffee on that windswept street corner that night in Toledo, Ohio, he didn't even know if I was Christian, let alone one being called by God to Bible school and beyond that, to the world. Brother Norvel laid hands on many people in the prayer line that night at Rhema, but when that anointing carried by the Apostle Paul went into me, he never knew what that would mean to all those I've had the honor and privilege to reach in the name of Jesus.

Everything this ministry has been graced by God to do from then until we leave earth, will be accredited to these unknown somebodies that God used to launch me into full-time ministry and beyond. Aside from Brother Norvel, these were just ordinary believers at the time they were used by God to get me into my lane to run my race. They had never passed out a tract, held a crusade, or written a book. They had never conducted a Bible study. They weren't ordained or licensed as an "officially recognized minister." At least as far as I know, they've done nothing other than obey God, allowing Him to use each of them in special and significant ways to minister to me at key points in my life. They'll all be rewarded just like every other unknown nobody that God needed to be an unknown somebody.

CHAPTER 24

WHOSE LINE WILL YOU STAND IN?

I had no idea what God had in store for me when I left the USA those many years ago. I flew away with $20 in my pocket and a one-way ticket to the Philippines, not knowing if anyone would be at the airport to meet me. When I arrived for the first time, I didn't know the language, and I didn't have any more than the promised monthly support from my mom and stepdad, and one small church in Toledo, Ohio, totaling $250. From September 1980 until now, I've been doing the Lord's work wherever He has sent me. Some time ago, the Lord told me that in our Philippine crusades I started in the fall of 1980, we had led more than 750,000 souls to Jesus. We've developed a thriving church network with hundreds of churches nationwide, and they're now reproducing my vision with crusades of their own. We have a Rhema Bible Training College in Ozamiz city, where hundreds of students have been trained and sent out to do their work for the Lord.

Thank you, Marilyn, for simply letting the joy of your salvation witness to Barbara, and bring her to the place in life where she was willing and ready to accept Jesus as Lord and Savior (Nehemiah 8:10;

1 Peter 1:8). I will be standing in your line as proof of your faithfulness to Jesus, rejoicing for all the rewards that will be given to you.

Thank you, Barbara, for being used by God to open my eyes to the true condition of my soul, and showing me the way to eternal life. You loved me enough to stay patient with me, doing your best to find a way to penetrate my hard, religious heart. I will be standing in your line as proof of your faithfulness to Jesus, rejoicing for all the rewards that will be given to you.

Thank you, Mac, for showing the kindness of God by buying me that cup of coffee on that cold winter's night in Toledo, Ohio. Your simple act of kindness was used by God to bring clarity with regards to His plan and purpose for my life and ministry from then on (Matthew 10:42). I will be standing in your line as proof of your faithfulness to Jesus, rejoicing for all the rewards that will be given to you.

Thank you, Norvel, for being an obedient ambassador and minister of the Full Gospel, laying hands on me in obedience to the leading of the Holy Spirit that night at Rhema. You didn't know who I was or what God had planned for my life, but because you did what He told you to do in that prayer line, a powerful anointing was imparted to me which I've carried ever since. I've also been led by the Lord to replicate this impartation to many over the years, in the same way you imparted God's miracle anointing me. As a result, I represent Jesus not just in word, but also in power (1 Corinthians 4:20). I will be standing in your line as proof of your faithfulness to Jesus, rejoicing for all the rewards that will be given to you.

MY LOVING WIFE, ETHEL

It would be remiss on my part if I didn't also take time to thank Ethel, my wife, for all the years of faithfulness to me as my wife, mother to our children, and helpmeet in this ministry. I met her almost immediately after arriving in the Philippines in September 1980, and we were married on May 7, 1983, in a big barn on a dirt floor up in the mountains of Mindanao, where her family was living at the time. I cannot imagine living these past decades of time without her at my side. She's perfect for me in every way a man could be blessed by his wife. I could write an entire book just about her, highlighting all the ways she's been there for me over and over again. I didn't know I needed her, but God sure did! He has used her to complete me as a man and minister. Thank you, honey, for being so wonderful in my life in so many ways, being my faithful, loving soulmate from the beginning until now, and beyond until Jesus returns. For sure, I will be the *first one* standing in your line as proof of your faithfulness to Jesus, rejoicing for all the rewards that will be given to you.

SO MANY OTHERS

These are just a few of the many believers who, over the years, have been instrumental in helping me obey God in ministry. There are many more lines I'll be standing in, to offer testimony for how they were used by the Lord in helping me be all I can be for Jesus. I think of Reverend Kenneth E. Hagin, founder of Rhema Bible Training College (whom we all just called Brother Hagin), and then his son and daughter-in-law, Pastor Kenneth W. and Lynette Hagin, who now oversee the worldwide Rhema ministry. I think of Rev. Kenneth Copeland, Rev. T.L. Osborn, Rev. Oral Roberts, Pastor John Osteen, Rev. Fred Price, Pastor Bob Yandian, and many others. Their books, sermons, and personal support were instrumental in my life's work for Jesus, and still are.

There are so many people God used to help me stay strong and true to His call. It's a great blessing to me in knowing that everyone who said or did something to help me along God's way will be recognized and rewarded for whatever I've done, or will do in the name of Jesus. This is what it means when you understand that one word: ENTRUSTED.

WHAT ABOUT YOU?

Whose lines will you be standing in? Who has been used by God to bring you to the Lord in salvation, and from then on, into a meaningful and fruitful life for Him? Our lives are but a vapor, that are here today and gone tomorrow (James 4:14). The people who were used by God to speak into your life understood what it meant to be entrusted with the gospel. They understood what is at stake for every human being after death, and the importance to seize every opportunity to reach out to those in need.

They didn't see your flaws or imperfections. They chose to see you through God's eyes—valuable and precious—a unique individual formed by His hand (Psalm 139:13-18). They didn't turn away in selfishness. They obeyed God and said what you needed to hear, and did what you needed them to do to keep you on the narrow way that leads to eternal life (Matthew 7:13-14). They share in your victories in battle. They share in your triumphs of faith. They have been your partners along life's way, injecting themselves into your life at key moments when you needed a word from God, a pat on the back, or even a stern rebuke.

They answered God's call the same way Isaiah did thousands of years ago in Isaiah 6:8. *"Here am I Lord, send me!"* It will be a great day of joy for you to stand in their line, and give witness to all the rewards they have earned. *You are part of what put value on their lives.*

CHAPTER 25

WALKING WORTHY

For this reason we also, since the day we heard it, do not cease to pray for you, and to ask that you may be filled with the knowledge of His will in all wisdom and spiritual understanding; **that you may walk worthy of the Lord, fully pleasing Him.**

—Colossians 1:9-10

A Christian's top priority in life should be to walk worthy of the upward calling, fully pleasing the Lord with the way we live our lives. Walking worthy means *fully* pleasing. Walking worthy some of the time, or most of the time, isn't good enough. Pleasing *partially* doesn't cut it. Of course, we know we're all works in progress, and make plenty of mistakes along life's way, but that's why God's mercy is new every morning (Lamentations 3:22-23).

This "priority mindset" isn't top priority with many believers, and that's a lifestyle they'll have to give an account for on the day they stand at the judgment seat of Christ. From God's perspective, the greatest tragedy on earth today is the lazy, lethargic, apathetic church. May it not be so concerning you—or me. In my prayer closet, I like to let the Lord know that in my opinion, it's the greatest honor of honors to represent Him here on earth. It thrills my soul to think that in some way I'm putting a smile on my heavenly Father's face! Things I'm doing. Things I'm thinking. Things I'm saying. How my life is more and more lining up with His Word. Expressing to Him a continued "attitude of gratitude," which we'll talk about in our next chapter. I'd like to think I'm giving Jesus a life He's satisfied with—a life that demonstrates an understanding of what it means to be entrusted with the gospel.

> I, therefore, the prisoner of the Lord, beseech you to **walk worthy of the calling** with which you were called.
>
> —Ephesians 4:1

The word "beseech" means "to plead," "to implore," "to urge," "to appeal," "to beg." Paul was pleading, imploring, urging, appealing, and even begging those Ephesian believers to get a clue, as we say. Unfortunately, there are still plenty of clueless Christians all around. What can we do? Be an example of the way things should be for those entrusted with the gospel.

FULLY PLEASING

> And say to Archippus, "**Take heed to the ministry** which you have received in the Lord, **that you may fulfill it**."
>
> —Colossians 4:17

> Paul, a bondservant of Jesus Christ, called to be an apostle, **separated to the gospel of God**.
>
> —Romans 1:1

WALKING WORTHY

We must be sanctified, separated, and different than the unbelievers. Why? For what reason? Because of the *honor* of representing the King of Kings and Lord of Lords. Because of the responsibility we have to share words with people in the name of Jesus—words that will give them the knowledge and awareness of what's waiting for them on the other side of physical death, should they choose to reject the love of God and free gift of salvation. Paul wanted Archippus to remember these things, because he himself was striving to live by them. The Holy Spirit wants us to remember as well. God wants us to "take heed" to the ministry, walking worthy of the calling and living a life that's fully pleasing in His sight.

This verse describes my life in Christ. I hope it describes yours as well. To be fully pleasing to Jesus, walking worthy of this high calling—that's what I live for. When I was meditating on this, the Lord gave me a simple statement which brought me clarity. He said, *"The plan is progress, not perfection."* God knows our frame. He knows our struggles. He knows what we do before we do it. He knows we all have issues with our flesh—some of us more so than others. Nevertheless, our intensity and drive to please Jesus becomes a spiritual force that no devil or demon can stand against. But if we don't set a high standard of excellence before the Lord, how are we to ever achieve the great things Jesus said we could do in His Name? We're *entrusted* with so much! The very least we can do is let our zealousness, drive, and intensity be our fortress, and at the same time, be the inspiration that others need to see.

That means we are ever vigilant with our day-to-day choices. We are always on the lookout for enemy activity against us. We are always scanning the horizon, ready to repel any attacks from the devil. We are alert and awake, with spiritual weapons in hand. We're like Nehemiah and his workers, who rebuilt the walls of Jerusalem with weapons in one hand and construction tools in the other (Nehemiah 4:17). We manage the clock, and do our best not to waste time pursuing the temporal things of this life at the expense of the invisible, spiritual, eternal things pertaining to God. *Above all, God is "beseeching" us to take time to meditate on the reality of eternity, and the two destinations for every created being.* I do this quite often, and you should, too.

We must always understand that as spirit beings, we will *never* cease to exist. Spirits don't die. They just keep on going, and according to the Word of God, obedience or disobedience to the Lord and His righteous standards will determine where all created spirits spend eternity. Some spirits have already made their choices and have had their eternal judgment sealed. Satan, demons and fallen angels all made the wrong choice. Angels in heaven made the right choice. Human beings have been given the power of choice as well, and God will honor whatever choices we make. He doesn't want anyone to die and go to hell, but He leaves it all up to us (2 Peter 3:9).

In all the books I've written, this issue of eternity is always included in whatever Bible topic God has me write about. This is what drives me and consumes me. It's wonderful beyond words to think about being with God, Jesus, the Holy Spirit and all the other godly saints and angels in heavenly bliss forever. Praise God forevermore! But once again, on the other side of that coin, I implore you use your imagination with regards to the destination awaiting all those who die without Jesus. What's it going to be like—for those suffering the wages of sin and rebellion against God? Imagine bobbing in a lake of fire and brimstone—the pain and suffering of it, along with the memory of a life spent rejecting God's offer of salvation. In Luke 16:19-31, Jesus tells the story of the rich man and Lazarus. That rich man is still looking for someone to touch his tongue with a drop of water—*but it will never happen.* There's no way you can overemphasize the horror of it. In short, Christians who truly understand the honor and responsibility of being entrusted with the gospel also understand the end game, and take heed to their ministries accordingly.

*Then I saw a great white throne and Him who sat on it, from whose face the earth and the heaven fled away. And there was found no place for them. And I saw the dead, small and great, standing before God, and **books were opened**. And **another book was opened**, which is the Book of Life. And the dead **were judged according to their works**, by the **things which were written in the books**. The sea gave up the dead who were in it, and Death and Hades delivered up the dead who were in them. **And they were judged, each one according to his works.** Then Death and Hades were cast into the lake of fire. And anyone not found **written in the Book of Life** was **cast into the lake of fire**.*

—Revelation 20:11-15

God wanted to make sure we would all know what happens to those who refuse to accept Jesus as Lord and Savior. There's a reason why the Book of Revelation is included in the whole of Scripture. Christians can do their best not to think about these things, but they do it to their own hurt. Just choosing not to think about something so terrible doesn't change a thing. This is what happens to every single soul from Adam until the end of time if they don't get saved. *This is where you and I would be going* if we hadn't responded to God's invitation and accepted the free gift of salvation in Christ Jesus. And once again, this is why being entrusted with the gospel is such an honor and such a great responsibility.

And once again, I ask the question; what can we do as believers in these last days? How can we exhort and encourage fellow believers to get in the game? *Be an example of the way things should be for those entrusted with the gospel.* Do in your life what Jesus did in His.

*And **for their sakes I sanctify Myself**, that they also may be sanctified by the truth.*

—John 17:19

CHAPTER 26

THE THANKFUL HEART

*In those days Hezekiah was sick and near death, and he prayed to the Lord; and He spoke to him and gave him a sign. But Hezekiah **did not repay according to the favor shown him**, for his heart was lifted up; therefore wrath was looming over him and over Judah and Jerusalem.*

—2 Chronicles 32:24-25

Thousands of years ago, King Hezekiah failed to walk with a thankful heart, and the result was judgment upon him, the city of Jerusalem, and all of Judah. Think about that for a minute. An unthankful heart opens the door for demonic destruction—not just for the person who doesn't understand the importance of saying "thank you," but for others all around. That's a sobering revelation. I've said this over and over, but I'll say it again: *being entrusted by God in these ways is the greatest honor and responsibility any Christian could ever have.* We need to be thankful for it, every day of our lives. If we don't cultivate a thankful heart, the same thing that happened to King Hezekiah will happen to us.

AVOID THE ATTITUDE OF INGRATITUDE

This attitude of ingratitude wasn't just a problem for King Hezekiah back then. Unfortunately, it's also a sign of the end-times now.

> *For since the creation of the world His invisible attributes are clearly seen, being understood by the things that are made, even His eternal power and Godhead, so that they are with excuse, because, although they knew God, they did not glorify Him as God, **nor were thankful**, but became futile in their thoughts, and their foolish hearts were darkened. Professing to be wise, they became fools. . . .*
>
> —Romans 1:20-22

To say the least, there are many "wise fools" all around us. According to this passage in Romans, it's clear that ingratitude and an unthankful heart mark the beginning of a progressive walk away from God. Hezekiah found this out the hard way, as do many today.

> *But know this, that in the last days perilous times will come: for men will be lovers of themselves, lovers of money, boasters, proud, blasphemers, disobedient to parents, **unthankful**, unholy. . . .*
>
> —2 Timothy 3:1-2

Prophetically, Paul knew things about the days in which we live now. What God showed him is supposed to give us fair warning about what to expect just before Jesus returns. In the last days there will be *perilous* times. That means dangerous times abound—times which will try and tempt us to compromise our walk with God. But the Lord in His mercy has clearly described the characteristics of the ungodly so we can identify and resist them at every turn. Among many that are listed, notice that an unthankful heart is included.

THE THANKFUL HEART

THIS IS WHAT GOD EXPECTS

> *Then as He entered a certain village, there met Him ten men who were lepers, who stood afar off. And they lifted up their voices and said, "Jesus, Master, have mercy on us!" So when Jesus saw them, He said to them, "Go, show yourselves to the priests." And so it was that as they went they were cleansed. And one of them, when he saw that he was healed, returned, and with a loud voice glorified God, and fell down on his face at His feet, **giving Him thanks**. And he was a Samaritan. So Jesus answered and said, "Were there not ten cleansed? **But where are the nine?** Were there not any found who returned to give glory to God except this foreigner?" And He said to him, "Arise, go your way. Your faith has made you well."*
>
> —Luke 17:12-19

The Holy Spirit inspired Luke to record this incident for at least five separate reasons, all of which we need to understand today if we're to comprehend the awesome honor and responsibility of being entrusted by God as we've been. Let's see what they are.

First, how did Jesus know all ten had been healed? Their miracle manifested as they went away to do what Jesus told them to do. Even though He wasn't physically present when the ten miracles of healing took place, Jesus knew they got their answer because they followed His instructions in faith—the same way we believe and receive today, when we pray and believe the answer is ours, according to Mark 11:24 and 1 John 5:14-15.

Second, only one out of ten realized it was more important to go back and say, "thank you," than to continue to the priests with the other nine healed lepers. Perhaps he intended to show himself to the priests after he took time to express his gratitude to the Lord, but we'll never know for sure. What we do know is that his heart was so full of thankfulness, he *had* to immediately come back to say, "thank you." And as we see from our Lord's response to the healed leper, that's more important to God than in keeping a long list of religious requirements. Because of this decision to return as he did, Jesus told him to *go his way* and forget about seeing the priests. This shows us his grateful, faithful heart superseded any religious duties he needed to perform, even though those duties were lawful and proper in the broader context. Jesus and His disciples upset the religious people at other times in the same way. Here's an example:

> At that time Jesus went through the grainfields on the Sabbath. And His disciples were hungry, and began to pluck heads of grain and to eat. And when the Pharisees saw it, they said to Him, "Look, Your disciples are doing what is not lawful to do on the Sabbath!" But He said to them, "Have you not read what David did when he was hungry, he and those who were with him; how he entered the house of God and ate the showbread which was not lawful for him to eat, nor for those who were with him, but only for the priests? Or have you not read in the law that on the Sabbath the priests in the temple profane the Sabbath, and are blameless? Yet I say to you that in this place there is One greater than the temple. But if you had known what this means, **'I desire mercy and not sacrifice,'** you would not have condemned the guiltless. For the Son of Man is Lord even of the Sabbath.
>
> —Matthew 12:1-8

This was a constant issue Jesus had with the religious people of His day. They were far more concerned with the outward works of religion, than with the inward attitudes of the heart. They were also far more concerned with outward *appearances* than with inward *attitudes*. As the

THE THANKFUL HEART

Lord told Samuel when he stood before the sons of Jesse to select a king to replace Saul, He selects and uses people based not upon how they may appear physically, but upon how tender and thankful their heart is towards the things of God (1 Samuel 16:1-12).

The takeaway from these Old Testament exchanges is obvious if we protect our thankful heart as entrusted ambassadors for Christ (2 Corinthians 5:20). We must always prioritize the giving of thanks to God whenever He does what He does to bless us and use us for His glory. That shows where our heart is, and reveals our awareness that being entrusted with God's Word and weapons is something we can never take for granted, or be ungrateful for. That is always more important to God than anything else. King David was well aware of this, even though he made plenty of major mistakes in life. That's why he's still called a man after God's own heart (Acts 13:22).

Third, because God has entrusted us with everything we need to operate effectively inside the Body of Christ, don't be embarrassed to acknowledge what God does for you when you walk by faith and not by sight (2 Corinthians 5:7). The healed leper proclaimed his miracle *loudly* and *publicly*, giving God glory. He didn't care who liked it or who didn't, and he wasn't the only one highlighted over this issue in the Word of God. There were others who had the same attitude after receiving their miracle. In John's gospel, not only was Jesus persecuted by the Pharisees for healing a blind man on the Sabbath day, but so was the blind man (John 9: 1-41)! In Luke's gospel, a crippled woman was immediately healed while Jesus was teaching in the synagogue, and Jesus was persecuted by the synagogue's ruler for performing the miracle on the Sabbath (Luke 13:10-17). And the religious persecution went right on after Jesus had left and gone back to heaven. In Acts Chapters 3 and 4, when Peter and John raised up a man crippled from birth in the name of Jesus, they were arrested, put in jail, and threatened with severe punishment if they continued preaching in the name of Jesus (Acts 4:16-22).

Fourth, the healed leper made sure Jesus knew he was thankful. He came back just so he could tell Him face to face. In like manner, our prayer times should always reflect a thankful heart (Philippians 4:6), not just because we're seeing wonderful results from our ministry work, but because we're entrusted to be used by God in the first place, even though we're all working to be more Christ-like ourselves!

Fifth, and most importantly, even though Jesus never told the ten lepers to return after they got healed to say, "thank you," His questioning as to the whereabouts of the other nine obviously tells us that God expects it.

> *Enter into His gates **with thanksgiving**, and into His courts with praise. **Be thankful to Him**, and bless His name. For the Lord is good; His mercy is everlasting, and His truth endures to all generations.*
>
> —Psalm 100:4-5

ALWAYS BE THANKFUL

> *Rejoice always, pray without ceasing, **in everything give thanks**; for this is the will of God in Christ Jesus for you.*
>
> —1 Thessalonians 5:18

No matter who, what, when, or where, God tells us to remain thankful each and every day. Those who understand the awesome honor and responsibility that goes with being entrusted with the things of God know this. Notice carefully the Word of God doesn't tell us to be thankful *for* everything, but to be thankful *in* everything. There is a big difference between those two responses.

We live in a cursed world that is run by a renegade spirit named Satan, and he is the god of this world (2 Corinthains 4:4). Stealing, killing, and destroying is what he does—against every human being, but especially against believers entrusted with the gospel. We don't give thanks for what the devil or his human puppets do or try to do. We give thanks that in the midst of these tests and trials, we know we've been entrusted with the authority to use the name of Jesus to successfully overcome each and every attempt by the devil to hurt, harm, or destroy us. Never forget; even though we are spiritually positioned far above every demon and devil out there in Christ (Ephesians 1:22; 1 John 4:4), we will still be attacked, and the more we do for the Lord, the more we'll be attacked. God's Word makes it clear—suffering for righteousness is acceptable with God while we live on earth (1 Peter 4:12-16). In all of this—the good, bad and ugly—we are to give thanks *and count it all joy*, because that's our faith in operation, and that's the only thing God responds to (James 1:2-5; Hebrews 11:6).

APPRECIATE EVERY GOOD GIFT

Don't waste time thinking or worrying about what you don't have. That only breeds fear for the future. Instead, discipline yourself to always think about all that you do have—and maintain a consistent attitude of thankfulness and gratitude. Every day is a gift from God—an opportunity to let God shine through you. On the spiritual side of things: thank God for your salvation, for the baptism of the Holy Spirit, the gifts of the Holy Spirit, the Lord's forgiveness when we ask, and His mercy which is new every day. Thank Him for angels assigned to assist and protect us. Thank God for the weapons of war, as describes in Ephesians Chapter 6. Thank Him for every good and perfect gift (James 1:17). And once again, thank Him for entrusting us with the one message that can save a soul from hell.

> *Oh, that men would give thanks to the Lord for His goodness, and for His wonderful works to the children of men.* **Let them sacrifice the sacrifices of thanksgiving**, *and declare His works with rejoicing.*
>
> —Psalm 107:21-22

Thousands of years ago, the psalmist wrote Psalm 107, inspired by the Holy Spirit. It's a dedicated declaration of thanksgiving—an attitude that, for the most part, is non-existent in the hearts and lives of millions of people, including many Christians.

In this life here on earth, we should thank Him for the necessities of life we have each day. Food, shelter, clothing, and whatever else we use and enjoy. The Bible says in Psalm 37:4, that if we delight ourselves in the Lord, He will give us the desires of our heart, as long as those desires line up with His desires for each of us. To be delightful with the Lord is to be thankful to the Lord. There is no "delight" unless there is thankfulness. The United States, as we know it today, has become the world's most prosperous and powerful nation. One of the national holidays Americans celebrate annually is called Thanksgiving Day, which is held every November. While most everybody takes the day off to celebrate this holiday with family and friends, very few really understand the circumstances that led to the first Thanksgiving ceremony hundreds of years ago.

In September 1620, a group of 102 passengers, known as Pilgrims, left England for the "New World," as they described it. More than anything else, they were seeking a place where they could freely worship and practice their Christian beliefs, which was forbidden by the Church of England. Arriving 66 days later in November 1620, after a treacherous ocean crossing in their tiny ship called the *Mayflower*, they suffered through a terrible winter that took a heavy toll on the settlers.

In addition to the brutal weather, they faced sickness and a dwindling food supply. By the time spring came, only 50 of the original 102 Mayflower passengers had survived. In November 1621, after the Pilgrim's first corn harvest was successful, Governor William Bradford organized a celebration that lasted three days. It was their way of thanking God for their blessings, but it was also a time of prayer and hope for better days ahead.

In spite of their hardships and difficulties at the beginning, they understood the importance of recognizing God as the sole source of supply, and that remains the key to the prosperity and success of *any nation*. Be sure to protect a thankful heart, because whether it be a nation or an individual serving God, *you will lose what you're not thankful for!*

THE THANKSGIVING DECLARATION

Let the redeemed of the Lord say so, Whom He has redeemed from the hand of the enemy.

—Psalm 107:2

Verse 2 from Psalm 107 is one that most charismatic and Pentecostal Christians know, quote, and declare often. No doubt, it's a powerful truth we need to cherish and live by. We are the redeemed, and we should be declaring that consistently. That's why this theme of thankfulness is repeated throughout Psalms 107.

In verse 1: *Oh, **give thanks to the Lord**, for He is good! For His mercy endures forever.* In verse 8: *Oh, that men would **give thanks to the Lord** for His goodness, and for His wonderful works to the children of men!* In verse 15: *Oh, that men would **give thanks to the Lord** for His goodness, and for His wonderful works to the children of men!* In verse 21: *Oh, that men would **give thanks to the Lord** for His goodness, and for His wonderful works to the children of men!* In verse 31: *Oh, that men would **give thanks to the Lord** for His goodness, and for His wonderful works to the children of men!*

Do you think the Holy Spirit is trying to get something over to us here? I think so! Anytime God repeats Himself five times in one psalm, its rather obvious He thinks the point should be well taken! Our lives need to be in a continuous "thanksgiving mode." This is one of the main reasons why David was called a man after God's heart. *At midnight I will rise **to give thanks to You**, because of Your righteous judgments* (Psalm 119:62). When we go to bed, how many of us set the alarm for midnight, just so we can hop out of bed and spend time thanking God for his mercy that endures forever, and for His wonderful works to the children of men? Not many, if any. Of course, there are always plenty of excuses for a lack of thankfulness, but none will hold any water with God. In fact, when things aren't going well and everything is falling apart, that's the *best time* to offer up thanksgiving *by faith*.

THE SACRIFICE OF THANKSGIVING

Psalm 107:21 declares the importance of giving thanks to the Lord, as do the four other verses in the same Psalm. But verse 22 is not to be overlooked. It talks about *the sacrifice of thanksgiving*. *"Oh, that men would give thanks to the Lord for His goodness, and for His wonderful works to the children of men! Let them **sacrifice the sacrifices of thanksgiving**, and declare His works with rejoicing"* (Psalm 107:21-22). What does that mean? It means the same thing as Hebrews 13:15: *"Therefore by Him let us continually offer **the sacrifice of praise** to God, that is, the fruit of our lips, **giving thanks** to His name."*

THE THANKFUL HEART

There are plenty of times in our lives when we don't feel like praising or expressing thankfulness to God. But that's a part of what it means to walk by faith and not by sight (2 Corinthians 5:7). The Bible talks about lifting up holy hands in prayer (1 Timothy 2:8). That's when we do it because it's the right thing to do, no matter how we may feel at the moment. At all times, God is worthy of our praise, and He's worthy of our thankfulness.

> And when they had laid many stripes on them, they threw them into prison, commanding the jailer to keep them securely. Having received such a charge, he put them into the inner prison and fastened their feet in the stocks. But at midnight Paul and Silas were **praying and singing hymns to God**, and the prisoners were listening to them.
>
> —Acts 16:23-25

What a great example of offering the sacrifice of praise and thanksgiving! Paul and Silas had *many stripes* laid upon their backs. That's the same type of torture they used on Jesus during His crucifixion ordeal. Consider this as well—afterwards they had no medical treatment for their wounds. No bandages. No pain pills. No aspirin. No morphine. Nothing. After they were whipped until their backs were nothing but bleeding strips of flesh hanging over exposed muscle and bones, they were thrown into a pitch dark jail cell in the inner depths of that prison, immobilized because their feet were secured in the stocks. There were probably rats, crawling insects, mosquitos, standing water on the floor, and whatever else could be in there to torment them in the dark. *If these two men could sing, praise, and offer thanks to God in the situation they were in, you and I have no excuse not to do the same whenever and wherever!*

Notice what happened when they did what they did. God sent an earthquake at midnight, that shook the jail's foundation—and that building's foundation only. No other nearby structure was damaged or affected. The earthquake opened all the jail cells, not just the one that Paul and Silas were in. Every prisoner in the prison had chains fall off from their hands and feet, and they were free to escape, but they didn't run! Why? Because Paul and Silas were not ashamed to praise and thank the Lord loudly in the midst of their trial. Their praise and worship became such a divine magnet, nobody wanted to leave!

When all the doors were opened and all the chains fell off, not only did Paul and Silas remain in their cell, but so did all the other prisoners. They had the chance to escape but they didn't. They were so enamored with the loud singing and praising from these two men, they just wanted to stay and hear some more. *Amazing!* The jailor and all his family got saved, and God only knows how many of the prisoners got saved as well. We'll meet them in heaven someday soon, and they can give us a head count! This is what sacrificial thankfulness and praise can do!

DECLARE GOD'S GREATNESS

> *Yours, O Lord, is the greatness, the power and the glory, the victory and the majesty; for all that is in heaven and in earth is Yours; Yours is the kingdom, O Lord, and You are exalted as head over all. Both riches and honor come from You, and You reign over all. In Your hand is power and might; in Your hand it is to make great and to give strength to all.* **Now therefore, our God, we thank You and praise Your glorious name.**
>
> —1 Chronicles 29:11-13

We are to declare God's greatness, glory, victory, and majesty. He's exalted over everything, and rules and reigns uncontested. He is our

THE THANKFUL HEART

source for all prosperity and honor. He imparts His power, might, and strength to all of us. Therefore, we thank Him and we praise Him. How often? All the time. Consistently. Faithfully. Without hesitation. Without apology. No matter what is going on in our lives that seeks to discourage us from doing these things—we do them anyway.

Almighty God has chosen to entrust us with everything needed to win the lost to Jesus. A thankful heart is one such weapon. Let's be sure our hearts are filled with nothing but thankfulness and praise. God deserves nothing less.

CHAPTER 27

INTENSITY IS INSPIRATIONAL

*So it was, when the Philistine arose and came and drew near to meet David, that David **hurried and ran toward the army** to meet the Philistine.*

—1 Samuel 17:48

Being zealous for God isn't just for our benefit. Others can be inspired by our passion in serving the Lord Jesus Christ—and they should be! This battlefield encounter between David and Goliath is a classic example of this. Read the entire seventeenth chapter of First Samuel, and you'll understand how quickly things change when even one man or woman of God has the faith and courage to face the impossible—and prevail. When it came time to engage the giant Goliath, David didn't try to swing around and attack from the rear. He didn't try to hide behind trees or rocks. He didn't approach with great caution and stealth. No! He ran right at him! He charged into the fight. And I especially appreciate how the Holy Spirit described this. Not only did David run right at the giant—it says he ran toward the entire Philistine army that was behind the giant. Praise God! It's no wonder God called David a man after his own heart (Acts 13:22).

> *And when the Philistines saw that their champion was dead, they fled. Now the men of Israel and Judah* **arose and shouted, and pursued the Philistines as far as the entrance of the valley and to the gates of Ekron.** *And the wounded of the Philistines fell along the road to Shaaraim, even as far as Gath and Ekron.*
>
> —1 Samuel 17:51b-52

Look what happened when the Jews saw what David did. They stood up and charged down the mountain, shouting and screaming at the enemy. They chased them with a vengeance, killing them as they went. When they were done annihilating the enemy, they returned and plundered their tents.

WHAT TOOK SO LONG?

Saul's army hid behind rocks and trees for 40 days, shaking in their boots for fear. In verse 19, the Bible says Saul and his army were in the Valley of Elah, *fighting with the Philistines*. They weren't fighting. They were hiding in fear! Not just fear, but terror. *"And all the men of Israel, when they saw the man, fled from him and were dreadfully afraid"* (1 Samuel 17:24). Twice a day, Goliath walked defiantly into the valley and challenged Saul and all the children of Israel. He taunted them. He mocked them. He challenged them. Nobody would dare volunteer to fight against this man. After all, this giant was really *big!* Depending on your translation of choice, he stood anywhere between 9.5 and 11 feet tall. He was a warrior from his youth and had killed many in battle. In addition, he had an armor bearer who carried his shield in front of him (verse 41).

INTENSITY IS INSPIRATIONAL

Eighty challenges were issued. Twice a day: morning and evening. Nobody had the courage to engage this man in a fight to the death—until David showed up with provisions for his brothers. Once David heard challenge #81, he went berserk with rage and indignation. He couldn't believe this situation was being tolerated. There was a holy anger that rose up in him. Long story short; he told King Saul he would be *eager* to confront and kill this man, and went down into the valley and did it. When that happened, look at how his intensity and faith inspired the army. All of a sudden, they were on their feet, charging the enemy without fear. They could've done this 40 days before, but they didn't because no one had the intensity in faith to inspire them.

You and I—we need to let our intensity inspire other believers around us. God has entrusted us with this charge. So what if people get offended with our passion and fervor for the Lord. We're not answering to them someday in heaven. When did Saul's army rise up and rout the enemy? When they saw what they saw. It says that when the Philistines *saw* that their champion was dead, they fled. And when the Jews *saw* the same thing, they were inspired to engage the enemy fearlessly.

KEEP KILLING THE ENEMY

Then David put his hand in his bag and took out a stone; and he slung it and struck the Philistine in his forehead, so that the stone sank into his forehead, and he fell on his face to the earth. So David prevailed over the Philistine with a sling and a stone, and **struck the Philistine and killed him.** *But there was no sword in the hand of David. Therefore David ran and stood over the Philistine, took his sword and* **drew it out of its sheath and killed him,** *and cut off his head with it.*

—1 Samuel 17:49-51

I want you to see something that most people overlook when reading this passage. The Bible says that David threw the stone and hit the giant square in the forehead with such force, the stone actually sunk into the man's skull. When that happened, he fell to the ground—dead. It plainly says David struck the Philistine with the stone *and killed him*. So, he's already dead. But David wasn't finished. He wanted to make a bold statement to both armies that day.

Notice the word "therefore" in verse 51. Because he was dead there wouldn't be any need to do anything else, right? David could've walked away at that point, and the victory would've been won. But no, he wanted to make a statement. *After he was already dead*, David ran and stood over the dead body (no doubt the armor bearer had already fled for his life). He took the giant's sword out of its sheath, *and killed him again!* Do you see that? He didn't need to do that, but he *wanted* to do that! What is he doing? He's sending a message to the enemy: *if you mess with the children of God, we're not just going to kill you; we're going to make an example out of you.* In essence, David was saying: *we can kill you today, and we can kill you anytime we want, and we'll keep on killing you as a sign and signal to all.* After David killed the giant with the stone, he ran to the dead body and used his own sword to run him through to make a "statement" to both armies. Then, as if that wasn't enough, he used the same sword to cut the giant's head off! He still wasn't done making his victory statement.

> *And David **took the head** of the Philistine and **brought it to Jerusalem**, but he put his armor in his tent.*
>
> —1 Samuel 17:54

Now that's what I call *inspired intensity!* When David showed up with food for his brothers, Saul was King and leader of the army. But when the army saw David do what he did, that was the end of King

INTENSITY IS INSPIRATIONAL

Saul's reign. David didn't officially become King of Israel until years later, but in the hearts and minds of the soldiers, David became their King that day.

> Not that I have already attained, or am already perfected; but I press on, that I may lay hold of that for which Christ Jesus has also laid hold of me. Brethren, I do not count myself to have apprehended; but one thing I do, **forgetting** those things which are behind and **reaching forward** to those things which are ahead. **I press toward the goal** for the prize of the upward call of God in Christ Jesus. Therefore, let us, **as many as are mature, have this mind**; and if in anything you think otherwise, God will reveal even this to you.
>
> —Philippians 3:12-15

We all know Paul had "skeletons in his closet." At one time, he was probably the most feared zealot against Christians and the gospel. But when he met Jesus on the Damascus Road, God changed his heart, changed his name, and sent him out to become one of most effective apostles of the early church. As such, he knew the success of his ministry would depend on three things which he shared with the Philippians. *First*, he had to forget his past. *Second*, he had to reach forward to things ahead. *Third*, he had to press towards the goal. If I may say it this way: he had to *press on, press through, and press in*. Spiritual intensity makes it possible to consistently do all three. God is no respecter of persons (Acts 10:34). By the grace of God Paul did it, and we can do it too (1 Corinthians 15:10).

> The law and the prophets were until John. Since that time, the kingdom of God has been preached, and everyone is **pressing into it**.
>
> —Luke 16:16

*And from the days of John the Baptist until now the kingdom of heaven suffers violence, and the violent **take it by force**.*

—Matthew 11:12

That word "pressing" in Luke's gospel is a word that screams "intensity." It means that no matter how severe the tests and challenges are in this life as a front-line soldier in God's army, we can make it. We can triumph in every situation, if we keep our heads and purpose in our hearts to forcefully and violently breakthrough in Jesus' name. This is not passive Christianity. This is intense, aggressive, in-the-devil's-face kind of Christianity. We take from the kingdom of darkness what we want and what we need for Jesus in ministry whenever we want, because we're the "Stronger Man" of Luke 11:21-22. The "Strong Man" is the devil, and he can't stop us. Why? Because in Christ, with the Holy Spirit living inside of us, we're stronger than he is. We press on. We press through and we press in—violently if necessary. (*for more detailed teaching on the Stronger Man, read my book, *You Can Be Who You Already Are*.)

SATISFACTION AND DISATISFACTION

I am satisfied with who Jesus is and what He did for me. You should be too. He was the pure and perfect Lamb of God, and He took away both the sin and the sins of the world (John 1:29; 1 John 2:2). He lived his life on earth without one spot, blemish, or sin. I find that absolutely amazing, given the fact that the devil did everything he could think of to try and trip Him up. Oh yes, I'm extremely and deeply satisfied in the work of My Savior. We all owe Him our very lives, because He was, and is, the Savior for all who wish to receive Him as Lord.

On the other hand, even though I'm totally satisfied with Jesus as Lord of my life, I'm *dissatisfied* with myself. What does that mean? It

INTENSITY IS INSPIRATIONAL

means I'm a work in progress, just like we all are. Remember what Paul told the Philippians. He said this about himself: *"Not that I have already attained, or am already perfected."* In other words, he knew he wasn't perfect before the Lord. If you read Romans Chapters 6, 7, and 8, you can get an idea of how he struggled with his own flesh, as we do as well with ours. All that being said, *we must have a holy dissatisfaction in our lives*. We can never settle for mediocrity. Jesus said He will vomit out of His mouth those whom He calls *lukewarm* (Revelation 3:16). Being some kind of "Sunday Morning Christian" doesn't cut it. We've got multitudes of people claiming to be Christian, who think like, act like, and talk like any rank-and-file unbeliever. You can't tell them apart from people lost in sin and on their way to hell.

Jesus wasn't like that. He was different. When He stepped into someone's synagogue, people just took a step back. He commanded their attention and respect. He knew Who He was, and lived that way from start to finish. Following in our Lord's footsteps, our intensity should drive us to improve each day before the Lord. We should strongly desire to get better at blessing, pleasing, and satisfying our God. No, we can't achieve perfection in this life, because our dead-to-sin flesh, the world's system, and the devil himself will always create problems. But we can choose to continue on the *journey* towards perfection, which will someday take place at the rapture, when our bodies are changed and the curse of sin removed (1 Corinthains 15:52; 1 Thessalonians 4:13-18).

ANOTHER SPIRIT

One of my favorite Bible characters in the Old Testament is Caleb, who was one of twelve spies Moses sent into the Promised Land to find out who and what was over there. Read Numbers Chapters 13 and 14. Twelve spies were sent in to spy out the land. Two of them, Joshua and

Caleb, came back with a good report of faith. The other ten came back with an evil report of unbelief. Listen to how God describes Caleb in the midst of all of this:

> But my servant Caleb, **because he has a different spirit in him** and has followed Me fully, I will bring into the land where he went, and his descendants shall inherit it.
>
> —Numbers 14:24

Caleb had a "different spirit." That simply means his attitude wasn't like most others. He was bold. He was aggressive. He was not afraid to risk offending people. He decided to intently follow God, and let the world beware. Fast forward 45 years later, and as Joshua is in the process of dividing up the Promised Land amongst the 12 tribes, Caleb comes along with some reminders to Joshua.

> **You know the word which the Lord said to Moses the man of God concerning you and me in Kadesh Barnea.** I was forty years old when Moses the servant of the Lord sent me from Kadesh Barnea to spy out the land, and I brought back word to him as it was in my heart. So Moses swore on that day, saying, 'Surely the land where your foot has trodden shall be your inheritance and your children's forever, because you have wholly followed the Lord my God.' And now behold, the Lord has kept me alive, as He said, these forty-five years, ever since the Lord spoke this word to Moses while Israel wandered in the wilderness; and now, here I am this day, eighty-five years old. **As yet I am as strong this day as on the day that Moses sent me; just as my strength was then, so now is my strength for war, both for going out and for coming in.**
>
> —Joshua 14:6b-11

INTENSITY IS INSPIRATIONAL

This man remembered the promise of God for forty-five *years*, and quoted it back to Joshua word for word. He did this without the benefit of printing presses, digital content in the "cloud," or Bibles everywhere in dozens of translations. For over four decades, he kept God's Word deep within his heart. He did this while wandering with all the unbelieving Jews in the desert, even though he and Joshua had stood their ground in faith those many years before. Caleb kept the faith, all the while watching tens of thousands of Jews die off one-by-one as they wandered aimlessly as punishment for their unbelief. *Intensity will give you the ability to do such a thing.* So, what was the outcome for all of this? Let's find out!

> *"Now therefore, **give me this mountain of which the Lord spoke in that day**; for you heard in that day how the **Anakim were there**, and that the cities **were great and fortified**. It may be that the Lord will be with me, and I shall be able to drive them out as the Lord said."*
>
> —Joshua 14:12

When the time came to pick his parcel of property in the Promised Land, he didn't pick the golf course villa. He didn't pick the house on the beach. He didn't pick the mansion on a hill. He wanted the mountain. Why? Because the giants were still up there, and he still wanted to fight them! He didn't get the chance back in Numbers Chapters 13 and 14 because of the fear and unbelief of those ten other spies, but now he has the opportunity to finally face them and destroy them. That doesn't make him fearful. Instead, it makes him excited. Just like David running at the giant Goliath, here we see Caleb eager to go up there—as an eight-five-year-old man—to kill the giants and take possession of the mountain. Who exactly was living up on that mountain? Let's find out!

And Joshua blessed him, and gave Hebron to Caleb the son of Jephunneh as an inheritance. Hebron therefore became the inheritance of Caleb the son of Jephunneh the Kenizzite to this day, because he wholly followed the Lord God of Israel. And the name of Hebron formerly was **Kirjath Arba (Arba was the greatest man among the Anakim)**. *Then the land has rest from war.*

—Joshua 14:13-15

The Anakim were huge giants, just like Goliath. When Goliath challenged the armies of Saul, his very presence terrified an entire army of Jews. Now here in this story, we see that up on that mountain, there isn't just one giant, there are fortified cities full of them (Numbers 13:28-33). And this "old man" is going to go up there and wipe them out—and he did! *Inspiring to say the least!*

INTENSITY OVERCOMES EXHAUSTION

One more example of how intensity does what only it can do can be seen in the life of Gideon, as described in Judges Chapters 6, 7, and 8. To summarize briefly here, Gideon was chosen by God to save the nation from a group of enemy kings who were invading the land (Judges 6:33). He sent out the call for all able-bodied men of military age to report immediately for duty to defend the nation, and they came—32,000 strong. But God told Gideon that there were *too many* soldiers for Him to use, so by a process of elimination, the large group got smaller and smaller. Judges 7:2-3 says that the first batch of soldiers sent home numbered 22,000, leaving 10,000 soldiers left. As if that wasn't concerning enough, God told Gideon there were still too many for Him to work His work. So, after they were tested by the way they drank at a nearby water source, 9,700 more soldiers were sent home. That meant Gideon

INTENSITY IS INSPIRATIONAL

ended up with only 300 men, against a combined force of 135,000 enemy soldiers (Judges 8:10). If I were Gideon, I might be looking for a clean pair of briefs right about now!

But by obeying God and doing exactly what he was told to do, Gideon and his 300 men prevailed with trumpets and lanterns. In confusion, 120,000 of the enemy killed themselves in the dark, and the remaining 15,000 were in full retreat, running for their lives (against just 300 soldiers—amazing!) This remnant also included several of the enemy kings who led the invasion. Gideon and his 300 men were in hot pursuit with an attitude that only an intense, passionate warrior for God can appreciate.

> *When Gideon came to the Jordan, he and the three hundred men who were with him crossed over, **exhausted but still in pursuit**.*
>
> —Judges 8:4

If you tell me that you're exhausted, you're telling me that you're so tired you can't go another step. You've reached your limit. You're unable to continue. Its more than just being tired. To be exhausted means to reach a point where you are finished. You're cooked. You're done. Well, that's exactly how Gideon and his 300 men were—exhausted. Exhausted from the battle in the middle of the night. Exhausted with the pursuit of the retreating enemy kings. Exhausted and ready to give up the pursuit. But they knew they had the enemy on the run, and they knew that now was the time to finish them off, lest they escape to fight another day. When they asked for some bread from the locals, they were refused service and assistance. So what did they do? They kept going, exhausted, *but still in pursuit*. Did they catch up with the enemy kings? Yes, they did, and they killed them. After that, they came back and "taught" the men of Succoth and Penuel never to refuse them again (Judges 8:5-9,16).

Intensity makes this possible! (*for more detailed teaching on this story, read my book, *You Can Be Who You Already Are*.)

According to 2 Chronicles 16:9, God looks for people across the world with whom He can show Himself strong to. In short, He's looking for someone with the intensity to say anything, do anything, or go anywhere in the name of Jesus. That's all on us. God doesn't make us intense. He doesn't shock us until we wake up to the reality of eternity in heaven or hell. He waits for us to make the choice. And when we do, understand that our intensity inspires others to raise their game as well. David did it. Caleb did it. Gideon did it. Paul, Peter, and the early church leaders did it. Most especially, Jesus did it. We can do it too. God is looking for a particular type of person to be strong to. Do you qualify?

CHAPTER 28

PROMISES TO LIVE BY

"His Lord said to him, '**Well done, good and faithful servant**; you were faithful over a few things, I will make you ruler over many things. Enter into the joy of your Lord.'

—Matthew 25:21

"His Lord said to him, "**Well done, good and faithful servant**; you have been faithful over a few things, I will make you ruler over many things. Enter into the joy of your Lord.'

—Matthew 25:23

For Christians who understand what it means to be entrusted with the life-changing message of the gospel, these are the words we want to hear in heaven. *This is our hope.* Someday in the not-too-distant future, we'll stand before the Lord Jesus to be judged for the lives we have lived, and the choices we have made. Rewards will be given proportionate to the levels of obedience exhibited.

I'm not competing with you, and you are not competing with me. We are all living and working for the Lord, and it's His approval that matters—no one else's. That's why it's important to remember that on that day when our works are judged, no two believers will receive the same rewards. Why? Because everybody is a unique creation by the hand of God. We are God's workmanship, and He doesn't create clones (Ephesians 2:10). From Adam until the end of time, believers have been living in different dispensations, in different parts of earth, experiencing different levels of resistance, undergoing various degrees of suffering and challenge. Each person responded to God in different ways with varying levels of obedience. That's why everybody's reward will differ from person to person. No two people have ever been identical, in what they faced fulfilling God's assignments and how they overcame the resultant adversity. Paul spoke about this in his letter to the Corinthains:

> *There are also celestial bodies and terrestrial bodies; but the glory of the celestial is one, and the glory of the terrestrial is another. There is one glory of the sun, another glory of the moon, and another glory of the stars; for one star differs from another star in glory.* **So also is the resurrection of the dead.** *The body is sown in corruption, it is raised in incorruption. It is sown in dishonor; it is raised in glory. It is sown in weakness, it is raised in power. It is sown a natural body, it is raised a spiritual body. There is a natural body, and there is a spiritual body.*
>
> —1 Corinthians 15:40-44

In the book of Daniel, we find that soulwinners will one day shine like the stars in the heavens (Daniel 12:3). As the universe is filled with stars that differ in brightness and glory, so too forever, believers will shine with God's glory differently from person to person. Therefore, we can all look forward to the day when we're rewarded in unique and wonderful ways, simply because we answered the call of Isaiah 6:8: *"Also*

I heard the voice of the Lord, saying: "Whom shall I send, and who will go for Us?" Then I said, "Here am I! Send me."

BUILD YOUR ETERNAL PERFORMANCE PORTFOLIO

As previously stated, we've been entrusted with free will. I made my choice many years ago, when I said to the Lord, "Here I am, I'm available. Use me and send me." And He has. If you do what I did, He'll do for you what He's done for me. In the world, when we decide to invest in the financial markets to make a profit, advisors encourage us to invest our money where there is a good track record of profitability. But when they do, they'll always tell you that past results do not guarantee future performance. They tell us this, so we understand the risk involved. That means profitability and the return on our investment isn't guaranteed. We could make a lot of money, but we also might lose it all. And if we do lose it all, they're not responsible for your loss. Answering the call to obey God is the opposite. When you build your eternal portfolio, you get blessed in this life *and* in the next (Matthew 6:30). There is no risk involved. So, be smart. Say "yes" to God, and live your life above the uncertainties of this world.

> "Do not lay up for yourselves treasures on earth, where moth and rust destroy and where thieves break in and steal; but **lay up for yourselves treasures in heaven**, where neither moth nor rust destroys and where thieves do not break in and steal. For where your treasure is, there your heart will be also."
>
> —Matthew 6-19-21

> So Jesus answered and said, "Assuredly, I say to you, there is no one who has left house or brothers or sisters or father or mother or wife or children or lands, for My sake and the

*gospel's, who shall not receive a hundredfold **now in this time**—houses and brothers and sisters and mothers and children and lands, with persecutions—**and in the age to come, eternal life**.*"

—Mark 10:29-30

When Jesus says, "Assuredly I say to you . . . ," that means your payday in heaven is guaranteed—where it really counts. In God's economy, past performance *does* guarantee future results!

In conclusion, let me repeat the verse quoted at the beginning of this book. It's something Jesus said, which is the truth we all must live by, now more than ever.

> "When someone has been given much, much will be required in return; and when someone has been **entrusted with much**, even more will be required."
>
> —Luke 12:48b NLT

Our life is a gift from God, and should be a gift to others. Prioritize the protection of these things that we've explored in this book. Nothing else matters. Nothing else is more important. Nothing else is necessary.

> *Hold fast the pattern of sound words which you have heard from me, in faith and love which are in Christ Jesus. That good thing which was **committed to you, keep by the Holy Spirit** who dwells in us.*
>
> —2 Timothy 1:13-14

> *. . . The glorious gospel of the blessed God which was **committed to my trust**.*
>
> —1 Timothy 1:11b

> *O Timothy! Guard what was **committed to your trust**, avoiding the profane and idle babblings and contradictions of what is falsely called knowledge. . . .*
>
> —1 Timothy 6:20

Entrusted for Eternity

We are entrusted to guard what has been entrusted. Be strong and do it! (1 Chronicles 28:10)

ABOUT THE AUTHOR

Mike Keyes grew up in Ohio and was raised in the Roman Catholic church. In 1973, he graduated from college to become a successful advertising executive and graphic artist. On September 21, 1978, at age twenty-six, he was born again and Spirit filled two days later. Immediately, the gifts of the Spirit began working in his life. Through his local church, he began to witness on the streets, in area prisons, and anywhere he could hand out tracts.

In September 1979, Reverend Keyes resigned his job to attend Rhema Bible College in Tulsa, Oklahoma, graduating in May 1980. In September 1980, he traveled to the Philippines with a oneway plane ticket, arriving without knowledge of the language or customs and with no one there to meet him. When he got off that plane to begin his ministry, he had twenty dollars in his pocket, one footlocker containing his Bible, class notes, a few changes of clothing, and the promise of support totaling $250 from no one except his parents and one small church in Toledo, Ohio.

From those humble beginnings and through his faithfulness to the calling of God over the years, the Lord has used Reverend Keyes extensively to reach untold numbers of people in the Philippines and around the world. Always emphasizing outreach to the remote, overlooked, out-of-the-way villages and towns that no one else has gone to, it is conservatively estimated that since the beginning of his ministry's outreach in 1980, over 750,000 souls have been won to Christ in his nationwide crusades in the Philippines.

Mike Keyes Ministries International (MKMI) is an apostolic ministry that reaches the lost, teaches the Christians, and trains the ministers. With a consistent crusade outreach, a church network of hundreds of churches, and the Rhema Bible College, Reverend Keyes and his staff, pastors, graduates, and students continue to fulfill the Great Commission wherever he is instructed to go by the Holy Spirit—throughout the Philippines and around the world.

Reverend Keyes is married to a native Filipina, Ethel, and has two children.

OTHER BOOKS BY
MIKE KEYES SR

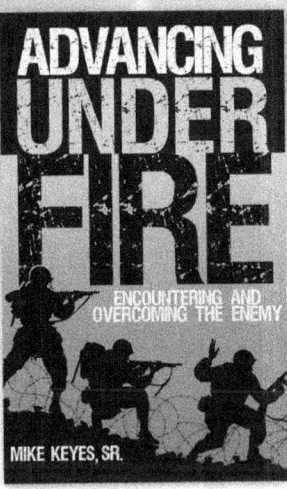

Advancing Under Fire
ISBN: 978-1-939570-47-5

In today's world there has been a gradual "slide" away from God and the things of God. What was once thought perverse and unthinkable is now thought to be the norm. Churches and ministers are bending over backwards to appease people calling their approach "user friendly" or "seeker friendly" not wishing to "offend" anyone. Advancing Under Fire challenges the Body of Christ to rise up, shed the mistakes and failures of the past and join forces to engage the enemy with the truth of the Gospel.

Divine Peace
ISBN: 978-1-939570-17-8

How can you live above fear and pressure and the frantic pace of life in these perilous times? *Divine Peace* reveals the principles of knowing and walking in God's peace every day and how to stand strong in the midst of every circumstance with a peace that passes all understanding.

OTHER BOOKS BY
MIKE KEYES SR

Be Strong! Stay Strong!
ISBN: 978-1-939570-00-0

God's perfect will is for every believer to be triumphant and victorious in life. *Be Strong! Stay Strong!* shares seven spiritual priorities and the importance of practicing them consistently, bringing any believer to the place of superior strength and victory over an attack of the enemy in these last days.

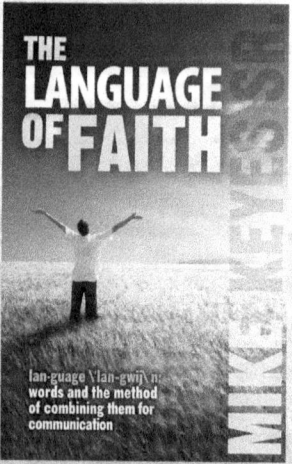

The Language of Faith
ISBN: 978-1-939570-02-4

Have you ever wondered how to communicate with God? In *The Language of Faith*, Mike Keyes, Sr. reveals the rules that govern the language of faith, how you can use those rules to speak faith, and as a result, see the windows of heaven open up on your behalf.

OTHER BOOKS BY
MIKE KEYES SR

Hope The Power to Believe Until You Receive!
ISBN: 978-1-939570-01-7

Have your hopes faded? Are you on the brink of compromise or defeat? Have you been crushed and believe there is no hope? REJOICE! THIS BOOK IS FOR YOU! As long as you're alive and can make a decision, THERE IS HOPE hope for recovery, restoration, and replenishment. Hope stirs nations to action. It keeps people sustained against unbelievable odds. Hope is God's agent of change. It brings joy in times of sorrow, light in times of darkness, and direction when confusion seems to reign. In this crucial teaching, Apostle Mike shares how you can regain hope and claim the victory!

You Can Be Who You Already Are
ISBN: 978-1-949106-11-4

This book is written with a sense of urgency unlike any other the author has written. You Can Be Who You Already Are has at its main core the purpose of helping believers fearlessly rise up in the midst of all the chaos around us and embrace the tremendous opportunities we have to win souls for Jesus in the last days. Many points or verses are repeated for emphasis to help us really grasp the truths presented through the repetition of certain passages, stories or examples found in scripture. You will be enlightened, reminded and encouraged to be who you already are in Christ. You can be the StrongerMan, members of God's congregation of the mighty. You can be who you already are!

OTHER BOOKS BY
MIKE KEYES SR

Crossing Over

When Jesus finished a day's worth of teaching ministry, He commanded His disciples to get into the boat and cross over to the other side of the lake. What does crossing over have to teach us today? Jesus wants us to cross over to the other side of ordinary, away from spiritual ignorance to a place of spiritual knowledge and awareness.

Determined Faith

Determined Faith shares five important keys to maintaining and strengthening your faith for the days ahead, followed by biblical examples of real people who chose to believe God and not give up. Determination is the attitude that refuses to tolerate laziness, lethargy, or apathy and triumphantly takes us from the beginning to the end in every fight of faith.

The Mandate of Must

The Mandate of Must identifies eight biblical mandates we must address and fulfill in these last days. They are commands from God and must be made top priority each day. By doing so, we allow God to be great in our lives, providing us with all the blessings to be prosperous, protected and successful.

The Radical Remnant

The world is growing darker by the day and many Christians have decided to compromise their faith for protection from persecution. Apostle Mike Keyes lays out the case for membership in God's Radical Remnant who refuse to compromise for anyone, anywhere, at any time.